TRICIA LOVVORN PATTERSON

THE UNWASTED LIFE

HOW TO LIVE A LIFE THAT MATTERS

TRICIA LOVVORN PATTERSON

DEDICATION

To my parents,
Mark & Patty Lovvorn.

You both have shown me what it looks like to live a life that matters. Thank you both for living a life centered on Jesus Christ.

Thank you for teaching me what it means to live a life of eternal significance. I am forever grateful for the example you have set for me.

CONTENTS

A NOTE FROM TRICIA

Dear friend,

Do you ever feel like you're wasting your life away? Do you feel like you're walking through life aimlessly, without a purpose? Do you feel like you were made for more, but you're not sure what the "more" entails? Do you desire to live with purpose & calling, but you don't even know what your purpose & calling really are? Do you want to live for something that will outlive your days here on the earth? Do you want to live a life worthy of your calling?

You are not alone.

The Unwasted Life unveils ten principles for living a life of eternal significance. In this study, I unfold the big-picture purpose & calling for every single believer, then I explicitly lay out the practical, daily applications to living out this grand, Kingdom focused life. If you desire to live a life that counts for something, then *The Unwasted Life* is for you!

Enter into eternal living. Live a life with eternal significance that will influence others far beyond these earthly days. Gain the confidence in knowing that at the end of your life, Jesus will undeniably say:

"Well done, my good and faithful servant."

Through this study, I am praying that you will gain a fire in your soul to live every day with passion, perseverance, and purpose. I invite you into daily Bible reading, reflection and response, fasting, and application each week in order to cause these principles to take root in your soul.

Please, don't waste your life away.

Join me in living a life unwasted.

For His Glory,

Tricia

INTRODUCTION

Every single time that I've taught a group on the topic of *The Unwasted Life*, I endure some kind of major spiritual warfare as I prepare. At first it caught me off guard. Now, it never does. Why? Because I believe wholeheartedly that the Enemy wants nothing more than to deceive us into wasting our lives away. If we can waste our lives away on the meaningless, fleeting things of this world, the Enemy is satisfied. His scheme is to pull us off course, cause us to drift, and distract us, so that we don't live out our God-given purpose. THAT is the reason, I always face spiritual warfare when I prepare to teach on this subject. It honestly fires me up, because I know that means LIFE-CHANGE is about to take place. He seeks to attack when he senses a threat, and YOU, my friend, are a threat. I am praying that you and I will live our lives as threats for the cause of the Kingdom! We want the Enemy shaking in his boots when he hears about our passion for Jesus Christ.

Will you join me in living a life that is a THREAT to the Enemy for the Kingdom of God in this world?

That's what this study is all about: living an unwasted life for the Kingdom of God – one that makes Satan tremble.

I remember as a high school student, I was struck to the core by this verse:

> *Ephesians 4:1 "I beg you to lead a life worthy of your calling, for you have been called by God."*

More than anything in life, I desire to live a life worthy of my calling, and that's what I desire for you.

As I studied this verse, I read a commentary that said that this idea of *worthy* means action that matches position. Because we have the position of sons and daughters of Jesus Christ, we should live a life that matches that calling.

"The believer who walks in a manner worthy of the calling with which he has been called is one whose daily living corresponds to his high position as a child of God and fellow heir with Jesus Christ. The Christian's practical living matches his spiritual position."

– John MacArthur

Does the way you live match your spiritual position as a son or daughter of the King?

I'm afraid many of us are living lives that have no evidence of our true position as children of the King of Kings and Lord of Lords. Sadly, many of us are living as if we have no sense of worth whatsoever.

Are you living a life worthy of your calling? Or are you living as if you're worthless without any sense of a calling?

Does your daily living match your position as a child of God?

Let's talk about what this kind of unwasted life looks like:

The Unwasted Life is NOT...

> The Striving Life

But... The Unwasted Life IS...

> The Surrendered Life

The unwasted life is less about *your* agenda of things *you* need to do, and more about surrender and abiding in Him daily and waiting to see all *he* will do through you.

The Unwasted Life is NOT...

> The Exhausted Life

But… The Unwasted Life IS…

The Self-Sacrificing Life

If following Christ isn't costing you something, then I'd challenge you to examine the way you follow Christ.

The Unwasted Life is NOT…

The Perfect Life

But… The Unwasted Life IS…

The Christ-Centered Life

The God-Honoring Life

The Spirit-Filled Life

The Unwasted Life isn't about *earning*. The Unwasted Life is about *abiding*.

I was recently looking back through my journals, and this entry jumped out to me:

"I don't want any 'lost years' of my life. I don't want to look back at the end of my life and say, 'if only...' I want to live with purpose, with meaning, with an impact on those around me for the kingdom of God." – February 22, 2012

This has been a constant prayer of my life, and I pray that it will become your prayer, as well.

PRAY
God, don't let me have any lost years of my life. I don't want to waste a single day that you've given me. Show me what it looks like to live with purpose for the Kingdom of God.

WEEK 1

THE UNWASTED LIFE

IS MARKED BY A

PERSPECTIVE OF THE

BREVITY OF LIFE

STUDY : : HEAD

Teach us to realize the brevity of life, so that we may grow in wisdom.

Psalm 90:12

In 2012, I was the Preschool Children's Coordinator at our church in Waco, Texas, First Baptist Woodway. Our pastor at the time was Pastor Mike Toby, an energetic, personable man, who I greatly admired. In October of that year, Pastor Toby became suddenly ill. What had begun with numbness in one of his hands developed into a diagnosis of incurable cancer. The news sent shockwaves through the church, but he asked our church not to pray for his health. Instead we were to pray that his passing would be painless and as easy as possible on he and his family. He explicitly expressed that he was ready to see his Savior face to face.

In November, just a month after his diagnosis, Pastor Toby filmed a video for our congregation. As he sat in his bed, no longer able to move, he brought a moving, unforgettable message to our church.

He explained to us that earlier that year, he had read the following verse in Psalm 90:12: *"Teach us to realize the brevity of life, so that we may grow in wisdom."* He said that looking back, he had no idea at the time how the Lord was preparing him for his last days here on this earth. The Lord had taught Pastor Toby the art of numbering his days. The Lord had given Pastor Toby the gift of living his days with a sense of urgency and purpose. Because of this, our pastor could say without hesitation, that he was ready to go home and see his Savior face to face.

He explained that he was confident that he had lived every day for the Lord, and he felt at complete peace knowing that he had lived his life with Jesus.

Every single day, Pastor Toby would wake up before dawn, spend time with Jesus, then go about his day completely on purpose for the Kingdom of God. In his final address to the church through his video, he explained that every night he could put his head on his pillow knowing with full assurance that he had lived his day for Christ.

He was ready. Pastor Toby passed away one short month later.

I'll never forget that message. His words have made an impact on me for the rest of my life. Am I living a life with such intentionality? Do I live every single day on purpose for the Kingdom of God? Do I live in a way that I would be ready? Do I live with confidence knowing that I haven't missed a life with and for Jesus?

Do you?

READ PSALM 39:4-7

"LORD, remind me how brief my time on earth will be. Remind me that my days are numbered — how fleeting my life is. You have made my life no longer than the width of my hand.

My entire lifetime is just a moment to you; at best, each of us is but a breath." We are merely moving shadows, and all our busy rushing ends in nothing. We heap up wealth, not knowing who will spend it. And so, Lord, where do I put my hope? My only hope is in you."
Psalm 39:4-7

This passage does not mean that your life is *insignificant* – it actually means the opposite, your life is *eternally significant*. That's why we don't want to waste it with all our "busy rushing."

With what "busy rushing" do you waste your life?

_____

_____

_____

_____

_____

Some people view the topic of the brevity of life as disheartening, but in the context of eternity it is not disheartening at all. The brevity of life becomes motivation for eternal living. In the context of our hope, maintaining a perspective of the shortness of our days here on earth, actually empowers us to live a more Kingdom-focused life.

For those of us, whose hope is in the Lord – our assurance is grounded & anchored in the reality of eternity with God. Therefore, we can live our earthly days with even greater abandon and freedom, because we know this is not our final home.

> *How would you describe the phrase: "we are merely moving shadows"?*

_____

_____

_____

_____

_____

The phrase "moving shadows" grabbed my attention in a way it never had before as I studied this passage not long ago. As I meditated on this passage, I caught myself analyzing the phrase as I played outside with my daughter one day.

My daughter, Joy and I were outside on a bright and sunny day. As my toddler and I danced around in the large shadows that day, Joy began asking questions about her shadow:

- What caused the shadow?

- Where did the shadow come from?

- Why was it so large?

- Why did it move every time she moved?

If you've ever played with a toddler, you know that the why questions can keep coming and keep coming. And this time, I welcomed all the "whys" because these questions allowed me to analyze this passage even more.

As I thought about the shadows, I began explaining that the sun was casting the shadow, and that the shadow was just a picture of our bodies. The shadow wasn't the real thing, just a picture.

Then, I thought about it in the context of this passage. This life is merely a "moving shadow" of the real life ahead of us in eternity with Christ.

A shadow is an illusion of the real thing. In this case, my time here on earth is merely a shadow compared to the real thing: my eternal life with Christ.

This thought brought me to Colossians 3:2-4.

READ COLOSSIANS 3:2-4

"Let heaven fill your thoughts. Do not think only about things down here on earth. For you died when Christ died, and your real life is hidden with Christ in God. And when Christ, who is your real life, is revealed to the whole world, you will share in all His glory."

What phrases grab your attention in this passage?

_____

_____

_____

_____

_____

Do you view <u>eternity</u> with Christ as your

real life?

Or, have you been like me at times and made the mistake of viewing life here on earth as the "main thing?" Don't get me wrong, the way we live our lives here on earth is very important. (That's the whole point of this Bible Study: to remind us how significant and vital it is to spend our days on this earth wisely.) But, if we miss this key truth: *that these days are like the snap of the fingers in comparison to eternity*, then we'll live for the wrong things. We'll live for fleeting, earthly things, rather than lasting, eternal things.

As I think about life here on earth as just a breath, just a moment, a moving shadow, I gain this sense of urgency to live out every single breath with eternal significance. What about you?

If my life is merely a moving shadow, then I want to cast a HUGE SHADOW for the Kingdom of Heaven during my life here on this earth.

And, remember: *The largest shadows are found where the light is shining brightest.*

As we walk in the light of our King, we will live our days here on earth, casting large shadows that display the reality of eternity with our God.

When we view this earthly life, in light of eternity, life becomes an *opportunity* to advance the Kingdom of God, rather than a compilation of fleeting, meaningless days.

Live with the end in mind.

WEEK 1
DAILY READING &
JOURNALING

Each day, answer the following questions as you journal about the passage for the day:

1. What does this Scripture have to do with this week's lesson?

2. In your own words, what is this Scripture saying?

3. How can this Scripture change the way you think?

4. How can this Scripture change the way you live?

Day 1	Read: Psalm 90:12
Day 2	Read: Psalm 39:4-7
Day 3	Read: Colossians 3:2-4
Day 4	Read: James 4:13-17

Day 5	Read: Philippians 3:19-20
Day 6	Read: Galatians 2:20
Day 7	Read: John 11:25

REFLECT :: HEART

"As long as you have breath in your body, you can breathe God's love into this world."

— Christine Caine

How does the topic of the brevity of life make you feel?

_____

_____

_____

_____

_____

Yes, our lives are "but a breath," but as believers, the breath in our lungs means that we have the privilege of declaring God's love to the lost world.

Do you feel a since of urgency to share God's love
with unbelievers? Why or why not?

_____

_____

_____

_____

_____

*"A Christian's goal is not to extend his days on this earth; a
Christian's goal is to spend every moment of every day for the
mission of advancing the Kingdom."*

– Afshin Ziafat

What do you focus on more:

Extending your days here on earth?

Or

Extending eternity for those who are lost?

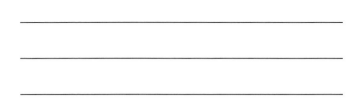

In the space below, color in the percentage of your life that you live for earthly, fleeting things rather than eternally significant things. Be honest.

All for the "earthly things"

In the introduction, I said:

> *"If following Christ isn't costing you something, then I'd challenge you to examine the way you follow Christ."*

On a scale from 1 to 10, how much are you willing to sacrifice for Christ?

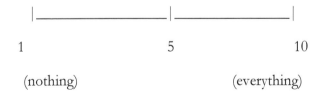

1   5   10

(nothing)   (everything)

When you get to the end of your life, what do you
want to be known for?

_____

_____

_____

_____

What do you give your life to that has no eternal
significance?

_____

_____

_____

_____

What do you give your life to that has complete eternal significance?

_____

_____

_____

What earthly illusions are you building your life upon right now? (i.e. fleeting success, fleeting popularity, fleeting power, fleeting materialism, fleeting appearance, etc)

_____

_____

_____

_____

Several years ago, I attended a Passion Conference in Houston. During the conference, Beth Moore spoke on the brevity of life. She asked everyone in the stadium to envision their headstone. She asked everyone to write down their full name, the day they were born, to place a dash, then leave a blank:

Tricia Lovvorn Patterson

May 16, 1989 – _____

Will you do the same?

_____

(your name)

_____ – _____

(your birthday)   (leave blank)

She asked each of us to circle the dash, and I'm going to do the same…circle that dash.

Then she asked us this question:

How are you going to live that dash?

_____

_____

How are you going to live during this short time on earth? What will that dash mean in your life?

When you get to the end of your life, when you see Jesus face to face, will you stand there knowing that you lived your "dash" well? Or will you wish that you had lived your days with more meaning? With more purpose? Will you wish that you lived for something of eternal significance?

When you get to the end of your life, and everything of this earth has faded away, what will remain? Will you have a life built on lasting, eternal things, or will you be left thinking: "Did I just waste my life away?"

HOW ARE YOU GOING TO LIVE YOUR DASH?

APPLY : : HANDS

"But whatever you do, find the God-centered, Christ-exalting, Bible-saturated passion of your life, and find your way to say it and live for it and die for it. And you will make a difference that lasts. You will not waste your life."

– John Piper

If you knew your life was going to end tomorrow, what 3 things would you want to do that you haven't done?

_____

_____

_____

_____

_____

_____

If you knew your life was going to end tomorrow,
who would you share the Gospel with?

_____

_____

_____

What's stopping you?

_____

_____

_____

Choose 1 thing to do this week that you listed above:

I plan to…. _____

_____

ELIMATING LIFE-WASTERS: WEEK 1: TIME-WASTERS

Each week, we will choose 1 thing to fast for 3 days.

This week, choose 1 <u>time-waster</u> to fast.

Examples: Social Media, Netflix binge-watching, etc.

(An aside about fasting: You should never fast a sin. We are to confess, repent of, turn from, and start living in freedom from sin. So, please do not fast things like: gossip, lying, cheating, worrying, etc. Those are all sins. You should fast the "extra" things in your life that you are willing to sacrifice for Christ and replace with more time with Jesus.)

For the next 3 days, I will fast…

_____

PRAY
Lord, give me a sense of urgency. Give me an eternal perspective. Help me see how short and fleeting life is in light of eternity. Help me live for things of eternal significance, rather than the things that will quickly fade away. My life is yours.

TRICIA LOVVORN PATTERSON

WEEK 2

THE UNWASTED LIFE
VALUES CHRIST
ABOVE ALL OTHER THINGS

STUDY :: HEAD

I consider everything a loss compared to the surpassing greatness of knowing Christ Jesus my Lord, for whose sake I have lost all things.

Philippians 3:8

As a Christian writer and speaker, I have to examine myself often. It's such a strange paradox. My life's goal is to make Christ known and to bring Him glory, but in order to do that I have to promote myself in order to get the message out. I'm told that I have to "build a platform" or "gain followers" just to get the message of Christ out to others, and to be honest, I have to check my motives *often.*

It's so easy to get caught up in the followers, the platform, and the self-promotion, and I have to constantly fight against anything being about *me.* I have to constantly ask myself: "Do I value *knowing* Christ more than anything else? Is my goal giving Christ glory or giving myself glory? Is my goal to make Christ known or make myself known?"

Here's a vulnerable admission:

> *I have to constantly examine myself to be sure that I value knowing Christ over being known.*

READ PHILIPPIANS 3:7-9

But whatever was to my profit I now consider loss for the sake of Christ. What is more, I consider everything a loss compared to the surpassing greatness of knowing Christ Jesus my Lord, for whose sake I have lost all things. I consider them rubbish, that I may gain Christ and be found in Him, not having a righteousness of my own that comes from the law, but that which is through faith in Christ – the righteousness that comes from God and is by faith.

Philippians 3:7-9

Are you like me? Do you struggle to make knowing Christ what you hold as supremely valuable above everything else? I *want* to make this the truth of my life, but I have to constantly destroy the idols and ulterior motives in my life, in order to keep Christ the supremely valuable prize of my life.

What does it mean to you to "know" Christ? To "gain" Christ? To be "found" in Christ?

_____

_____

_____

Can you say that you consider everything *rubbish* compared to knowing Christ?

_____

_____

_____

Be honest. What do you value above Christ?

- My accomplishments? My best efforts?
- My popularity? My status?
- My reputation?
- My number of followers?
- My American dream?

_____

_____

_____

Can you confidently say:

All those things I once wanted, all those things I once pursued, all those things I built my life on, I now count them a <u>loss</u> compared to the <u>surpassing value</u> of <u>knowing</u> Christ.

In this passage, Paul says: "For whose sake, I have LOST ALL THINGS."

Are you willing to lose it all for the sake of Christ? Are you willing to lay everything down in order to pursue Christ? Are you willing to surrender your life that much? Are you willing to say, "It's not about me. It's all about Christ."

Are you willing to lay down your life, in order to gain Christ?

I call it the *greatest exchange.* An exchange of life for life: Jesus Christ gave His life for me, now I give my life back in return.

READ PHILLIPIANS 3:4-6

"Though I could have confidence in my own effort if anyone could. Indeed, if others have reason for confidence in their own efforts, I have even more! I was circumcised when I was eight days old. I am a pure-blooded citizen of Israel and a member of the tribe of Benjamin—a real Hebrew if there ever was one! I was a member of the Pharisees, who demand the strictest obedience to the Jewish law. I was so zealous that I harshly persecuted the church. And as for righteousness, I obeyed the law without fault."

List the things that Paul once placed his confidence in:

_____

_____

_____

_____

_____

_____

> What's your list of accomplishments that you build
> your life upon?

_____

_____

_____

_____

Now, some of you might be thinking…

"I'm not like the rest of you. I don't have a list of successes, accomplishments, or popularity to hang my hat on. I just have a list of failures."

If that's how you feel, you are not alone.

Maybe instead of marking your life by a list of accomplishments, you're marking your life by a list of failures.

Listen: Measuring your life by the "accomplishments" column isn't going to amount to anything, and measuring your life by the "failures" column isn't either.

Here's the thing: Neither list holds any weight in God's eyes. As believers, we have to stop measuring and marking ourselves by the world's standards. We don't live by the world's measuring system, anymore!

These labels are not what define you. You are not marked by what you have done or haven't done, you are marked by what CHRIST HAS DONE on your behalf.

You are not found because of your successes, you are not lost because of your failures. All of it is a <u>loss</u> compared to knowing Christ and being <u>found</u> in Him.

Your worth is not based on your righteousness or lack thereof, but your worth is based completely on the righteousness of Christ, which He has *transferred* to each one of you.

Stop banking on your accomplishments. Stop sulking in your failures. We're operating with the wrong measuring system when we live by the accomplishment and failure columns.

The only thing you can bank on is the fact that you have been credited with the righteousness of Jesus Christ, and now you can be found in Him. So, erase your lists, and cover your life with the label: "Child of God."

Nothing else matters. Nothing else compares. Nothing else holds weight. Everything else is peripheral. It all fades away in the presence of Jesus Christ.

What I once considered a gain or what I was once *trying* to gain, I throw it all aside that I might gain Christ. Are you with me? Are you willing to let go of this world's standards, in order to take hold of Christ?

You can't straddle the fence when it comes to following Christ. You can't have one foot in both worlds. You cannot gain the world and gain Christ. You must choose one or the other.

WEEK 2
DAILY READING &
JOURNALING

Each day, answer the following questions as you journal about the passage for the day:

1. What does this Scripture have to do with this week's lesson?

2. In your own words, what is this Scripture saying?

3. How can this Scripture change the way you think?

4. How can this Scripture change the way you live?

Day 1	Read: Philippians 3:7-9
Day 2	Read: Philippians 3:4-6
Day 3	Read: Revelation 2:2-5
Day 4	Read: Jeremiah 2:2

Day 5	Read: Acts 20:24
Day 6	Read: Romans 8:18
Day 7	Read: 1 John 2:15-17

REFLECT : : HEART

"We can't live with one foot in the world and one in the Kingdom."

— Joyce Meyer

So where do you find yourself in all of this? Can you honestly say that <u>everything</u> is a loss compared to Christ?

Is he the sole one that you live for? Do you truly believe that nothing even compares to Jesus?

Are you willing to give up your list of successes and failures to say:

"None of it matters. The single thing I label myself with is Jesus Christ."

List of   List of Failures

Accomplishments

_____   _____

_____   _____

_____   _____

_____   _____

Now, write across those lists in bold:

CHILD OF GOD

What do you need to lose in order to gain Christ?

_____

_____

_____

APPLY : : HANDS

Each year, I ask God to give me a verse for that year. This year as I prayed over 2017 these are the verses He gave me:

"I know all the things you do. I have seen your hard work and your patient endurance. I know you don't tolerate evil people. You have examined the claims of those who say they are apostles but are not. You have discovered they are liars. You have patiently suffered for me without quitting. But I have this complaint against you. You don't love me or each other as you did at first. Look how far you have fallen from your first love! Turn back to me again and work as you did at first."

Revelation 2:2-5

In this passage, we see a church that would be considered the "doing church." Jesus says that He has seen their hard work, their good deeds, their diligence, but He had one complaint against them.

The complaint: "You've fallen from your first love."

When the Lord gave me this verse for 2017, it was like a convicting dagger to the heart. I'm just like this church. I'm a "doer" and a "striver" in my walk with Christ. I have the lists of accomplishments that I bank on, and the list of "to-dos" that I need to perform.

53

But, Jesus was convicting me and revealing the truth that I had begun "falling from my first love."

Remember, as I mentioned at the beginning of this week: I have to examine my heart constantly to be sure that I'm making Christ the central focus, rather than myself or *my* impact.

> *"Don't set your eyes on impact, but set your eyes on Jesus and knowing and loving Him more!"*
>
> – *Jennie Allen*

Are you like me? Have you gotten caught up in all that you can *do* for Christ?

God is tenderly whispering to your heart: "Don't get so caught up in what you can *do*. This is about *being with me*. You've gotten off track. Turn back to me. Come back to your first love."

I once heard an interview with Billy Graham, and this is what the interviewer asked: *Looking back over your life, do you have any regrets?*

And, Billy Graham's response is something I will never forget. He said: *I regret that I didn't spend more time with Jesus. I don't regret that I didn't take more speaking engagements. I don't regret not having a bigger ministry. I regret that I didn't know Jesus more.*

If this is true for Billy Graham, one of the greatest evangelists in all of history, then I am certain this is true for me. All the matters is knowing Jesus more.

We should not aspire after any other thing but to know and love Jesus.

Are you striving after something other than Jesus? Have you fallen from your first love and fallen for the lie that something else with satisfy?

What do you need to repent of today, in order to turn back to your first love?

_____

_____

_____

_____

What ONE action step can you take to prove that you value Christ over all things?

_____

_____

_____

_____

ELIMATING
LIFE-WASTERS:
WEEK 2: MONEY-WASTERS

This week, we talked about valuing Christ above all other things. One way that we see what we value most in life is through our bank-accounts. How do you spend most of your money? What are you willing to give up for the next 3 days that might be a "money-waster" in your life?

This week, choose 1 <u>money-waster</u> to fast for the next 3 days.

Examples: Shopping, Starbucks, etc.

For the next 3 days, I will fast...

_____

(A great way to take that "wasted-money" and use it for eternal purposes is by giving it to your local church or finding someone in need that could use your resources. Be a Kingdom steward of the earthly possessions God has given you.)

PRAY

Lord, reveal to me what I value more than you. Reveal to me what I love more than you. Reveal to me what I'm building my life upon other than you. Help me surrender my list of accomplishments and my list of failures. All I desire is to know you, to be found in you, and to gain you alone.
I want you above all things.
Here's my life, Lord. It's yours.

TRICIA LOVVORN PATTERSON

WEEK 3

THE UNWASTED LIFE
IS ONE THAT
ABIDES IN JESUS DAILY

STUDY : : HEAD

Abide in Me, and I in you. As the branch cannot bear fruit of itself unless it abides in the vine, so neither can you unless you abide in Me. "I am the vine, you are the branches; he who abides in Me and I in him, he bears much fruit, for apart from Me you can do nothing.

John 15:4-5

When I was in college, I had several distinct places where I met with God on the regular.

During my sophomore year of college, finding this place of solitude with God was shockingly easy because I found myself in a place of isolation and loneliness. During that year of college, I had roommates who distanced themselves from me, and it left me feeling extremely lonely while at home. As sad and pathetic as it sounds, I would retreat to my closet because I felt unwanted in my own living room. That closet became a very sacred place. That closet in a small house in Waco, Texas is the place where I met with God constantly. I can remember many days, sitting on the floor of my closet, crying from the pain of isolation, but finding almost tangible comfort from the presence of my loving God. Looking back at that house where I really didn't feel "at home," I strangely remember some of the sweetest times of feeling most "at home" in the presence of my God.

READ JOHN 15:4-8

Remain in me, and I will remain in you. For a branch cannot produce fruit if it is severed from the vine, and you cannot be fruitful unless you remain in me. "Yes, I am the vine; you are the branches. Those who remain in me, and I in them, will produce much fruit. For apart from me you can do nothing. Anyone who does not remain in me is thrown away like a useless branch and withers. Such branches are gathered into a pile to be burned. But if you remain in me and my words remain in you, you may ask for anything you want, and it will be granted! [8] When you produce much fruit, you are my true disciples. This brings great glory to my Father.

John 15:4-8

We often think of "the unwasted life" as the fruitful life. But, so often we bypass the source by which the fruit is produced.

If you want to live a fruitful life, you better be connected to the supply vine: Jesus Christ.

How do we connect with our "fruit supply"? We must purposely connect with Jesus on a daily basis.

What do you think this phrase: "abide in Me" means?

_____

_____

_____

The phrase "abide in Me" found in this passage means: to remain, to dwell, to live. The Message Translation puts it this way: *"Live in me. Make your home in me just as I do in you."*

As I thought about this phrase, "make your home in me," I thought back to that house on 3rd Street in Waco, Texas. That house where I felt so unwelcomed, and yet I found "home" in the presence of God. That's the place where I experienced this truth so deeply.

I once heard a missionary share that it didn't matter where in the world he was at the time, he could be thousands of miles away from family and friends, but he was able to find "home" in the presence of God.

You know the phrase, "Home is where the heart is." That's a sweet, sentimental phrase, but I think a more accurate phrase is: "Home is where the presence of God is."

Can you say that being with Jesus is where you are most at home?

Why or why not?

_____

_____

_____

_____

_____

This idea of abiding and dwelling in Christ sent me to *Psalm 27:4.*

READ PSALM 27:4

"One thing I ask of the Lord, this is what I seek most: that I may dwell in the House of the Lord all the days of my life, to gaze upon the beauty of the Lord and to seek Him in his temple."

The phrase, the "one thing I ask of the Lord" always strikes me when I read this verse. The ONE THING...

What's the *one thing* you ask of the Lord? Is it *to dwell in the house of the Lord all the days of your life?* If I'm 100% honest, no. This isn't usually what I ask of the Lord. I ask for loads and loads of other things, but simply asking Him that I may live in His presence all the days of my life is not what I commonly ask. I'm trying to change that.

I think many of us accept Christ as our Savior, then say, "I'll see You when this life is done. I'm going to pursue *my* plans. I'm going to pursue my American dream of the spouse, the two kids, the successful job, the Pinterest perfect home, etc, etc."

But what if the *one thing* we sought most in life, was to dwell in His presence?

- Not to live in comfort, safety, and convenience.
- Not to live in prosperity or gain success.
- Not to gain acceptance and popularity.
- Not to gain power and prestige.
- Not to satisfy our every whim and pleasure with earthly things.

What if we really lived as followers of Christ who wanted *one thing* in life: TO DWELL IN THE HOUSE OF THE LORD ALL THE DAYS OF OUR LIVES.

READ PSALM 27:8

Let's skip down just a few verses to Psalm 27:8:

"My heart has heard you say, 'Come & talk with me.' And my heart responds, 'Lord, I am coming.'"

Psalm 27:8

Our loving, always-available, open-armed God is beckoning us to come into His presence every single day. He says here in this verse, "Come and talk with me." He's gesturing us over and gently asking us to seek His face.

We are called to seek God's face; we are not called to seek His hand and all He can *do* for us or *give* to us. When was the last time you simply decided to seek His face, rather than seek *your* wish list?

I picture God our Father, crouched down, with arms wide open, like I stand when inviting my young daughter in for an embrace. He's crouched down, gesturing us over, inviting us to sit and talk with Him. Will our response be: "Lord, I am coming. Your face, Lord, is all I seek."

Often, we can find what we're seeking most in life based upon what we give our time to. Are you willing to sacrifice your own agenda to spend time with Jesus?

I have found this to be very true of my life: *What we give our time to proves what we love most in life.*

What do you seek most in life?

_____

_____

_____

_____

_____

To what do you give most of your time?

_____

_____

_____

To what do you give most of your thoughts?

_____

_____

_____

Let's head back over to John 15:

> *"Those who remain in me, and I in them, will produce much
> fruit. For apart from me you can do nothing."*

> *John 15:5*

What does it mean to you to produce much fruit?

The "unwasted life" is undoubtedly a life that bears fruit, right? We don't want to live fruitless lives. We want our lives to count for something. So, we can't miss this truth here in John 15:5. There's a condition to bearing fruit: you must abide in Christ. If you are not connected to Christ, you will not produce fruit.

Apart from Christ, you can do nothing. You've got no chance at producing an ounce of fruit, if you're not connected to Christ.

When you're disconnected from Christ, you're disconnected from the source of nourishment.

Jesus is the source by which we live the Christian life.

The wording here is significate:

All we can do apart from Christ is: nothing

Fruit is non-existent apart from Christ. You will live a *completely fruitless* life apart from Christ. Your life will never produce anything of significance apart from Christ. Everything you think you're producing will end up being worthless in God's economy apart from Christ.

Isaiah 64:6 explains the reality of this difficult truth even more:

"all our righteous acts are like filthy rags."

Even the "best" things we do – our most "righteous acts" are like filthy rags apart from Christ.

Although at first glance, this looks pretty hopeless and harsh, the reality is that this way of living is *freeing!*

We don't have to *do* enough. We don't have to *be* enough. Christ *already* has *done* enough. Christ *already* has *been* enough. This takes the pressure off. No, I can't produce anything on my own, but when I'm connected to Jesus…that's an entirely different story.

When I'm connected to Jesus, the producer of all fruit, my life will overflow with an abundance of fruit that I could have never produced in my own strength.

My simple role is connection to Jesus. My role is not the fruitfulness. Christ provides the fruitfulness. My role as the branch is connection to the source. *Connection to Jesus every single day.*

As I remain connected to Jesus Christ on a daily basis, I act as a branch, displaying the fruit from the work of the vine.

Heading back to John 15 one more time:

"If you abide in me and my words abide in you, ask whatever you wish, and it will be given you. This is to my Father's glory, that you bear much fruit, showing yourselves to be my disciples."

John 15:7-8

> How can God's word abide in you?

_____

_____

_____

_____

_____

We will talk in even more depth about spending time in the Word of God, because I am *very* passionate about this spiritual discipline. If we do not know the Word of God, if we do not spend time in the Word of God, we will not learn the voice of God. And, if we do not learn how to hear the voice of God, we will miss what it means to abide in Jesus.

> Do you believe that you can "ask whatever you wish, and it will be given you"?
>
> Why or why not?

_____

_____

_____

_____

_____

We know that everything in the Bible is absolutely true, so how come I haven't received every single thing that I've asked for when I pray? How can this verse possibly be true?

Here's how: There is a prerequisite to our asking. The prerequisite: abiding in Christ.

Why does this matter? Because when we abide in Christ, the nature of our asking changes. When you abide in Jesus, your will is aligned with God's will.

You begin asking for God's will to be done, rather than for *your* will to be done. And, as these verses say: This is all for our Father's glory.

Another verse that underscores this truth is found in Psalm 37:4...

READ PSALM 37:4

"Delight yourself in the LORD; And He will give you the desires of your heart."

Psalm 37:4

I've read this verse hundreds of times, but I read it wrong for many, many years. For years, I read it as: *If I spend time with Him, then, as a reward, He will give me the things I want.*

Now I read: *When I find Him as my sole delight, His desires become my desires.*

Not only is He the *fulfiller* of my desires, but He's the *creator* who plants new, different, God-like desires in my heart.

His desires become my desires. How? Because the *one thing I seek most in life* is to delight in Him, to abide in Him, to dwell with Him.

Our hearts change when they're connected to His heart.

———————————

Not long ago, I asked my Facebook friends: *"What is it that keeps you from living the unwasted life for Christ?"*

My friend Sari had a beautiful response:

"We all know that being close to Jesus is the safest place to be. I imagine in my mind's eye that I am walking so closely to Him that we bump against each other and that I could hold his clothing between my fingers without much effort. When I am distracted and leave that space, I miss out on so much. Not just the security, joy, contentment, and peace, but also opportunities to see people and life through His perspective. When I leave that space I lose my focus and fix my eyes on things of this world. In my life, I have to be intentional everyday to stay close to Jesus. In my heart, I have to cling to Him."

Well said, Sari. Well said.

WEEK 3
DAILY READING &
JOURNALING

Each day, answer the following questions as you journal about the passage for the day:

1. What does this Scripture have to do with this week's lesson?

2. In your own words, what is this Scripture saying?

3. How can this Scripture change the way you think?

4. How can this Scripture change the way you live?

Day 1	Read: John 15:4-8
Day 2	Read: Psalm 27:4
Day 3	Read: Psalm 27:8
Day 4	Read: Psalm 37:4

Day 5	Read: Colossians 1:10
Day 6	Read: Galatians 5:22-23
Day 7	Read: Matthew 6:33

REFLECT : : HEART

"A soul filled with large thoughts of the Vine will be a strong branch, and will abide confidently in Him. Be much occupied with Jesus, and believe much in Him, as the True Vine."

– Andrew Murray

Be honest with yourself:

What's the one thing you seek most in life?

_____

_____

_____

_____

What fruit do others see in your life that proves you are a disciple of Christ?

_____

_____

_____

_____

How often do you abide in Christ?

Mark where you belong:

| _____ | _____ | _____ | _____ |

Never   Almost Never   Sometimes   Almost Always   Always

APPLY : : HANDS

"Oh, that you would come and begin simply to listen to His Word and to ask only the one question: Does He really mean that I should abide in Him? The answer His Word gives is so simple and so sure: By His almighty grace you now are in Him; that same almighty grace will indeed enable you to abide in Him. By faith you became partakers of the initial grace; by that same faith you can enjoy the continuous grace of abiding in Him."
– Andrew Murray

List 4 ways you will abide in Christ this week:

1. _____

2. _____

3. _____

4. _____

Choose one verse to memorize and meditate upon as a way of allowing His words to abide in you:

I will memorize:_____

_____

_____

ELIMATING
LIFE-WASTERS:
WEEK 3: TIME-WASTERS

After discussing the importance of abiding in Christ, I thought focusing on time-wasters would be appropriate, once again.

Choose 1 time-waster to fast for the next 3 days.

Examples: TV, pressing the snooze button, Instagram, Facebook, etc.

For the next 3 days, I will fast...

_____

PRAY
Lord, I desire to abide in You. Make your presence evident to me, as I come before you. Reveal to me the things I seek in life besides you. I desire to seek you most in life. The one thing I ask is to dwell in your presence every single day. Lord, be the producer of fruit in my life as I remain connected to you. All for your glory.

WEEK 4

_____

THE UNWASTED LIFE

IS THE SURRENDERED

LIFE

_____

STUDY : : HEAD

If you refuse to take up your cross and follow me, you are not worthy of being mine. If you cling to your life, you will lose it; but if you give it up for me, you will find true life.

Matthew 10:38-39

As my friend, Sari, said in last week's lesson: *"In my life, I have to be intentional every day to stay close to Jesus. In my heart, I have to cling to Him."*

I love how she said she has to *cling* to Christ, because in all honesty, I tend to cling to loads of other things and people other than Christ. This word "cling" made me think of this verse in Matthew 10:39:

If you cling to your life, you will lose it; but if you give it up for me, you will find true life.

The Lord used this verse to grab ahold of my attention and truly change the trajectory of my life. I share the following story often, because this experience made a profound impact on the way I live my life:

Right after my husband and I got married, I went through a year-long battle with great anxiety, worry, and fear. I wrestled through a time where I was clinging so tightly to the lives of my husband, my family, and my own, that I was actually *paralyzed* to really live the life that God had set before me.

My husband, Sam, travels for work, and during these first years of marriage, I was consumed in the "what-if" world. "What-if" his plane goes down? "What if" something happens to him? "What-if" something happens to me? "What-if, what-if, what-if?"

This "what-if world" I was constantly living in was keeping me from living in the "what-is reality" of life, which caused me to truly waste away a year of life with worry and fear.

One day, I was lying next to Sam before he left town, literally clinging to him, and I remember praying and saying: "God, you can't let anything happen to him. He's *mine*." God spoke to my heart, clear as day and said: "Tricia, that's where you're wrong. He's not *yours*. He's *mine*."

That day, God began teaching me the process of "*loose-grip living*."

The Lord had to pry my white-knuckles off of my life. I had to hand my life over to Him, and trade in clinging to my life for clinging to Christ alone.

When I began trusting God with my life and surrendering my life to Him, I began to finally live the full life God intended for me to live.

You see, I was losing my life during that time. I was wasting away. But, when I began to give up the control of my life to Him, I found true life.

READ MATTHEW 10:37-39

If you love your father or mother more than you love me, you are not worthy of being mine; or if you love your son or daughter more than me, you are not worthy of being mine. If you refuse to take up your cross and follow me, you are not worthy of being mine, If you cling to your life, you will lose it; but if you give it up for me, you will find true life.

Matthew 10:37-39

Why would Jesus say "if you love your father or mother" or "your son or daughter more than me you are not worthy of being mine"? What does Jesus mean by this?

_____

_____

_____

_____

Do you have trouble accepting this teaching from Jesus? Why or why not?

_____

_____

_____

_____

What does it mean to "take up your cross"?

_____

_____

_____

_____

_____

> How might one "refuse" to take up his cross and
> follow Christ?

_____

_____

_____

_____

_____

> What does it mean to "give up your life" for Christ?

_____

_____

_____

_____

_____

You see, before I learned the lesson of "loose-grip" living, my life revolved around myself, my husband, and my family.

Now, my life is built on and around Jesus Christ, alone. *Everything else is an avenue by which I can live for Jesus.*

Now I can love my husband and treasure him as a *gift* given by God, rather than a *possession* that I cling to as my own. With Jesus as the center of my life, everything else becomes peripheral, and yet every other relationship improves. Let me explain how that's possible.

The love produced from my relationship with Jesus overflows into a greater love toward my husband. Now, I can offer a higher quality of love. This quality of love, overflowing from a constant, unconditional love from Christ, far exceeds the love that came when I was solely clinging to my husband.

Now I can raise my daughter, not as the center of my world, but as a treasure, that I have the honor of constantly pointing to the center of our world: Jesus.

Are you willing to surrender your life to God's control, and live a "loose-grip life" – fully abandoned to the God who is 100%, unquestionably, fully trustworthy?

Surrender has everything to do with trust. I think a lot of us have trouble surrendering, because we have trouble trusting. Maybe we don't truly believe that God is trustworthy.

If we truly trusted God, we would fully surrender to God.

The proof of genuine trust in God's sovereignty is laying your life at His feet. True trust means handing your life over to His control.

We all know the verse *Jeremiah 29:11:*

"For I know the plans I have for you, declares the Lord, plans to prosper you and not to harm you, plans to give you hope and a future..."

We all love this verse, and hang it on signs in our houses, but here's what we believe (especially in America): "His plans are to prosper me, so that means, I'll have the most successful job, the biggest house, the nicest car, the cutest/instagram-worthy family."

But, let's take a step back real quick...Do you know the context of this verse? This is written to exiles. To

God's people who were in captivity – away from their homes, away from all they had ever known, away from all they had ever dreamed their lives would be. This was not the plan any of these people had for themselves, and yet they could still trust God's plan for their lives.

Do you have that kind of trust in God's sovereignty? Even if His meaning of "prosper" is different from your meaning of "prosper?"

READ DANIEL 3:16-18

Shadrach, Meshach and Abednego replied to him, "King Nebuchadnezzar, we do not need to defend ourselves before you in this matter. If we are thrown into the blazing furnace, the God we serve is able to deliver us from it, and he will deliver us from Your Majesty's hand. But even if he does not, we want you to know, Your Majesty, that we will not serve your gods or worship the image of gold you have set up."

Daniel 3:16-18

When I think about a picture of surrendered lives, I often think of the three men in the fiery furnace. Shadrach, Meshach, and Abednego were unwilling to bow down to any god other than the One True God. They were willing to lay down their lives for God.

In anticipation of their fate, they boldly proclaimed:

Daniel 3:17 "If we are thrown into the blazing furnace, the God we serve is able to save us from it, and he will rescue us from your hand…but <u>even if</u> he does not, we will not serve your gods…"

God convicted me with this passage:

1. Do I have the faith and boldness to *believe* that He will save me?

2. *Even if* He doesn't do what I think He ought to, do I still trust Him?

> Do you have an "even-if" kind of faith?

_____

_____

_____

"Even-if" circumstances aren't what you expected, are you still able to trust Him?

I remember having an "even-if" moment several years ago. It was Tuesday, June 25, 2013. My mom went in for the dreaded colonoscopy… a very routine procedure, and all we were waiting to hear after the appointment was that everything looked normal.

As I sat at my kitchen table that morning, studying for the Bible Study lesson I would be teaching the very next day about idolatry, my dad called. With an eerily calm voice, he said, "Well, everything is fine, but they found a tumor." My heart sank, my breath gave way. "What?! A tumor?" He replied with the same calm tone, "Yes, they're doing a biopsy to see if it is benign or not. We'll find out tomorrow. They're confident that either way, she'll be fine. It's very treatable."

Not what I wanted to hear. Who ever wants to hear the word "tumor"? The next 24 hours were bathed in prayer. I couldn't figure out how to process this news. "See if it's benign or not...very treatable...." I could barely handle it.

But, my mom. My mom, the solid rock. No fear. No questioning. No doubts. Full confidence that whatever happened, He was in control and He is still good, no matter what. She was ready for the diagnosis to go either way. She was as calm and at peace as I had ever seen.

My admiration for my mom grew even more from Tuesday to Wednesday during that waiting period. And, because of the example of my mom, my confidence in the never-changing character of God became more solid than ever.

I remember studying the following verse in Job just before all of this occurred:

Job 2:10 "Should we accept only good things from the hand of God and never anything bad?"

As I meditated on this verse, I begged God for only the good.

Then as I drove to work the very next day, awaiting the results, I asked the Lord to speak to me through a song, and the next one that came on the radio was "Even If" ...Here are the lyrics:

> *Even if the healing doesn't come*
> *And life falls apart*
> *And dreams are still undone*
> *You are God You are good*
> *Forever faithful One*
> *Even if the healing*
> *Even if the healing doesn't come*
>
> *You're still the Great and Mighty One*
> *We trust You always*
> *You're working all things for our good*
> *We'll sing your praise*

What a reminder, but honestly not what I wanted to hear. "Even if the healing doesn't come" — hold on, what? Even if it doesn't come?

Could I still believe: "You are God, You are good, forever faithful One, even if the healing doesn't come…." I didn't have any other choice than to believe in and count on that Truth.

My "even-if" kind-of-faith was tested that week. I determined to place my faith in the never-changing God, rather than the ever-changing circumstances of the world. Yes, I determined to place my faith in Him…even if the healing didn't come.

I can thankfully say that the tumor was benign, but I know that is not the reality for many of you who have endured "even-if" moments throughout your life.

Are you able and willing to surrender all things for the sake of Christ? Do you trust Him enough to lay your life at His feet?

Our faith is not in the *outcome*, but our faith is in *Jesus Christ*, our Hope.

When you trust God enough to surrender your life to Him, you're guaranteed to live a life unwasted.

WEEK 4
DAILY READING &
JOURNALING

Each day, answer the following questions as you journal about the passage for the day:

1. What does this Scripture have to do with this week's lesson?

2. In your own words, what is this Scripture saying?

3. How can this Scripture change the way you think?

4. How can this Scripture change the way you live?

Day 1	Read: Matthew 10:37-39
Day 2	Read: Matthew 16:24-26
Day 3	Read: Hebrews 12:1-3
Day 4	Read: Luke 9:57-62

Day 5	Read: James 4:4-10
Day 6	Read: Daniel 3:17-18
Day 7	Read: 2 Corinthians 3:17

REFLECT : : HEART

"God wants us to find our satisfaction in Him rather than waste our time and effort on things that cannot satisfy. But when we look to other sources for satisfaction, we are guilty of idolatry."

– Beth Moore

When we're unwilling to surrender fully to the Lord, we're actually participating in idolatry.

For many of us, giving over the idols in our lives will be a process. A continual process that we must be constantly aware of. Idols have a way of creeping their way back in to our lives.

"Some of the idols in our lives – things or people we have put in God's place – can take much longer to remove. Some of them have been in those places for years, and only the power of God can make them budge. We must begin to remove idols by choosing to recognize their existence and admitting their inability to keep us satisfied." – Beth Moore

I want you to examine your heart and ask the Holy Spirit to reveal the things in your life that you need to surrender. Ask him to show you the ways that you might be "losing your life" as Matthew 10:29 says.

> What are the idols in your life?
>
> (What is that main thing that is taking your attention from the one true God? What is that thing that is keeping you from living fully for Him?)

[Circle the answers that apply]

Possible Idols:

- Security, Comfort, Convenience

- Financial Stability, Greed, Materialism

- Desire for Attention, Affection, Acceptance

- Approval, Relationships, Popularity, Romance

- Safety, Control

- Plans, Achievements, Goals, Accomplishments, Success

- Family, Friends, Marriage

- Food

- Physical Appearance

- Yourself

(other)_____

_____

_____

Could you possibly be idolizing one (or more) of these things, and in the process might you be losing your life? Idolizing means that you love something more than God. That's exactly what Matthew 10 says:

If you love your father or mother more than you love me, you are not worthy of being mine; or if you love your son or daughter more than me, you are not worthy of being mine. If you refuse to take up your cross and follow me, you are not worthy of being mine, If you cling to your life, you will lose it; but if you give it up for me, you will find true life.

Matthew 10:37-39

> What is it in life that you love more than God?

_____

_____

_____

_____

Are you willing to lay down that idol, in order to find true life in Christ?

How will you surrender your idol(s) today?

_____

_____

_____

_____

_____

_____

THE ULTIMATE SURRENDER

Before we move forward, I want to stop right here. Some of you may be reading this, and you have never made the decision to give your life to Christ. You've never made Jesus Christ the Lord and Savior of your life. If that is you, I want to invite you into the life-changing, eternity-altering decision to ask Jesus to be the Savior of your life.

I want to be blunt: Without Jesus Christ, you <u>will</u> *waste your life*. Without Jesus Christ, you will miss what life is truly about. Without Jesus Christ you will never reach heaven. If you don't have a relationship with Jesus, don't miss this opportunity to change your life for eternity. If you know something is missing in your life…if you feel like you're wasting your life today…don't miss this time of response.

Scripture tells us that if we confess with our mouths that Jesus is Lord, and believe in our hearts that God raised Him from the dead, we will be saved. It's that easy! Salvation has nothing to do with our own works or how "good" we are, but it has everything to do with the grace of God demonstrated through the death and resurrection of Jesus Christ.

If you have decided to make Jesus your Lord, respond by filling in the statement below:

I, _____, make you, Jesus, the Lord and Savior of my life. I believe that you died on the Cross to save me from my sins. I believe you were raised from the dead. I believe you are alive. I believe that through you, I have been forgiven of all my sins. I believe that through you I have eternal life. I believe that through you, my debt has been paid, and I have been covered with the righteousness of Christ. I am saying, "YES" to you today, Jesus. Thank you for saving me. Thank you for making me new. Thank you for dying in my place. Thank you for taking on the punishment that I deserved. Thank you for giving your life as a substitute for mine. I'm giving my life to you in return. I will love you and follow you forever. My life is yours.

Signature:

_____

Date: _____

As a disclaimer: No, you do not have to sign and date an agreement to seal your salvation experience, but I find this to be such a special, tangible reminder. I hope that you never question or doubt the decision that you just made, but if you ever do, I pray that you will look back at the paragraph above and gain the confidence and assurance that your salvation is certain and your eternity is locked in place.

For those of you who have made the decision to follow Christ:

You have made the ultimate decision of surrender. You have given your life to Christ. Nothing can ever alter this decision. Be sure of that. But, each day, you must make the decision to surrender your will, your plans, your desires to the lordship of Jesus Christ.

The title "Lord" means master. As believers, we make Jesus the master of our lives. He is in control. But, many of us (myself included) have a difficult time

handing over the full control of our lives. This is
where daily surrender enters in.

Do you trust God's control and plan for your life? Do
you trust His plan even if it's much different than
your own?

Why or why not?

_____

_____

_____

_____

What are the circumstances that you need to lay at
His feet & trust Him with?

_____

_____

_____

_____

Is there something you're clinging to that's keeping you from living the "loose-grip" kind-of-way?

_____

_____

_____

_____

Where do you find yourself on the spectrum of surrender?

0 = I'm a total control freak and cannot give up the control of my life.

5 = Can't we share the control, God?

10 = Here's my life! I hand it over in full surrender to You, God.

|__|__|__|__|__|__|__|__|__|__|

0   1   2   3   4   5   6   7   8   9   10

APPLY : : HANDS

"Great people don't do great things. God does great things through surrendered people."

— Jennie Allen

I'm a big believer in physically demonstrating our surrender through posture. I believe when we take a physical posture, our heart follows closely behind.

This week, I challenge you to pray each day in one of the greatest postures of surrender: **lying prostrate on the ground.**

Day 1 Prayer	Reveal to me what I'm trying to control in my life.
Day 2 Prayer	Give me the power to let go of control.
Day 3 Prayer	Show me the idols lurking in my life. What do I love more than you, God?

Day 4	By Your power, dethrone the idols in my heart.
Day 5	Give me the "even-if" kind of faith.
Day 6	Teach me the art of "loose-grip" living.

ELIMATING
LIFE-WASTERS:
WEEK 4: MATERIAL-
WASTERS

This week's fast will be focused on the material-wasters in our lives. Fasting is one of the most tangible practices of surrender that we can participate in. What are you willing to give up, in order to give yourself to God more fully?

Choose 1 <u>material-waster</u> to fast for the next 3 days.

Examples: Give up shopping. Give away some of your belongings, etc.

For the next 3 days, I will fast…

_____

PRAY

All to Jesus I surrender
All to Him I freely give
I will ever love and trust Him
In His presence daily live

All to Jesus I surrender
Humbly at His feet I bow
Worldly pleasures all forsaken
Take me Jesus take me now

I surrender all
I surrender all
All to Thee my blessed Savior
I surrender all

All to Jesus I surrender
Make me Savior wholly Thine
Let me feel the Holy Spirit
Truly know that Thou art mine

All to Jesus I surrender
Lord I give myself to Thee
Fill me with Thy love and power
Let Thy blessings fall on me

All to Jesus I surrender
Now I feel the sacred flame
Oh the joy of full salvation
Glory glory to His name

(*I Surrender All*)

WEEK 5

THE UNWASTED LIFE

IS MARKED BY A CONTINUAL

HUNGER FOR GOD

STUDY : : HEAD

You must crave pure spiritual milk so that you can grow into the fullness of your salvation.

1 Peter 2:2a

Have you ever seen those snickers commercials where the characters turn into alternate personalities when they're hungry? "You're not you, when you're hungry. Snickers Satisfies." Did you ever imagine that those commercials could have spiritual implications? Well, they most definitely do!

Those commercials completely personify me when I haven't filled my hungry soul with God's Word. Only He can satisfy, and when I turn to anything else to fill my empty soul, I always come up short, and I'm always left living with this alternate, old-natured personality.

I am absolutely not the person God wants me to be when I haven't spent time in His presence every day. Anyone else out there experience this? I literally feel like two different people depending on if I have spent time in the Word or not.

When I let His character inform my character on a daily basis, my attitude is transformed. But, when I neglect spending time in the Word, I become a reflection of anything and everything around me other than Jesus.

We must gain a heart that craves and hungers after God on a daily basis. If we do not gain this heart of hunger for our satisfying God, we will turn to the junk of the world to fill our empty souls.

READ 1 PETER 2:2-3

You must crave pure spiritual milk so that you can grow into the fullness of your salvation. Cry out for this nourishment as a baby cries out for milk, now that you have had a taste of the Lord's kindness and goodness.

1 Peter 2:2-3

What is the "pure spiritual milk" Peter is encouraging us to crave?

_____

_____

_____

_____

What does it mean to you to "grow into the fullness of your salvation" – what might that look like in your life?

_____

_____

_____

_____

If you find yourself sitting there, thinking: "I just don't hunger for Him. I don't have that craving in my soul." You're not alone. Most likely, you've trained yourself to crave after the things of this world, rather than God. You have bought into the lie that the junk of this world will satisfy, but it leaves you crashing and empty each and every time.

Let's think about it in this way:

You can live your whole life eating junk food. You'll find yourself constantly hungry because the food you're putting into your body isn't ever truly satisfying. The sugar and junk you're eating leaves you crashing and needing more, so you continually go back for more: constantly snacking on the unsatisfying junk food that your pantry or nearest drive-thru has to offer.

Or, you can become disciplined. You can instead, turn to the satisfying, good, healthy food. The food that really fills and sustains you. When you turn to the good food, not only are you satisfied each and every day, but you also feel the long-term effects. You experience the positive results of eating in a healthy manner, and this healthy lifestyle overflows in every other aspect of your life.

On the other hand, if you continue down the road of unhealthy eating, not only do you feel tired, sick, and dissatisfied on a daily basis, but you also experience the negative repercussions of this lifestyle long-term. You gain weight, you're more likely to experience disease, you're unable to participate in the activities you'd like to be a part of, and on and on.

The same principle is true in our spiritual lives. If we neglect filling our hungry souls with the only truly satisfying, nourishment that comes from God's Word, then we will find ourselves lacking in the riches of God's goodness. If we fill ourselves with the scraps of this world, then the effects will be: lack of joy, happiness, fulfillment, and wisdom. And instead we'll gain: burdens, baggage and the inability to live out the life that God has for us.

Listen: You are training yourself to crave *something*. You will either crave after the riches of God or you will crave after the scraps of this world. What are you training your hungry soul to crave?

If you find yourself lacking in your hunger for God: just have a taste.

READ PSALM 34:8

"Taste and see that the Lord is good…"

Psalm 34:8

The more and more you go to His Word, the more you will train yourself to crave it. If you've never had a taste of His Word, how could you possibly hunger after it?

I remember when I was younger, I was repulsed by guacamole. I could not understand anyone who liked it! Then, one day, a friend asked me if I had ever actually tried it. I sheepishly admitted that I had not. So, she dared me to take a bite. Y'all…my life was forever changed. I cannot get enough of guacamole!

I think a lot of us are doing the same thing with God. We just don't understand how His Word could really satisfy. It's like we're looking in from the outside, and we're just baffled at the thought. If that's true for you, here's my dare: *Have a taste*.

I guarantee that once you have a taste of God's Word, you'll see just how good He really is, and you will gain an insatiable hunger for more and more of Him.

Once you begin filling yourself with God's Word, you will find yourself craving for Him every single day. And, on those days that you neglect being with Him, you will feel the effect. You will feel the hunger pangs of missing your time with God.

That is the mark of a mature believer. The believer who craves after God on a daily basis, and when she hasn't been with Him, the hunger pangs strike, because she has trained herself to need Him each and every day.

WEEK 5
DAILY READING &
JOURNALING

Each day, answer the following questions as you
journal about the passage for the day:

1. What does this Scripture have to do with this week's
   lesson?

2. In your own words, what is this Scripture saying?

3. How can this Scripture change the way you think?

4. How can this Scripture change the way you live?

Day 1	Read: 1 Peter 2:2-3
Day 2	Read: Hebrews 4:12
Day 3	Read: 2 Timothy 3:16-17

Day 4	Read: Psalm 119:105
Day 5	Read: Matthew 7:24
Day 6	Read: Psalm 63:1-8
Day 7	Read: Psalm 36:7-9

REFLECT :: HEART

"A believer should count it a <u>wasted</u> day when he does not learn something new from or is not more deeply enriched by the truth of God's Word. Scripture is food for the believer's growth and power – and there is no other…The church cannot operate on truth it is not taught; believers cannot function on principles they have not learned. The most noble are still those who search the Scriptures daily."

– John MacArthur

I'm afraid we have many malnourished believers, who are neglecting spending time in the Word of God. As followers of Christ, we should consider is a wasted day, when we do not spend time in His Word.

Let's spend some time honestly evaluating how we're doing in our time alone with God…

How often do you spend time in the Word of God?

1. Never

2. Several Times a Year

3.   Once a month

4.   Over once a month

5.   Once a week

6.   3 Times a Week

7.   Daily

1	2	3	4	5	6	7

If you want to hear and know the Voice of God, you have to read and know the Word of God.

Remember: *What we give our time to proves what we love most in life.*

What is it that's keeping you from spending time with God each day?

_____

_____

_____

_____

What have you trained yourself to crave each day?

(i.e. social media, attention, popularity, possessions, food, achievement, accolades, etc.)

_____

_____

_____

_____

APPLY : : HANDS

"If we don't feel strong desires for the manifestation of the glory of God, it is not because you have drunk deeply and are satisfied. It is because we have nibbled so long at the table of the world. Our soul is stuffed with small things, and there is no room for the great." – John Piper

What if, over the next week, you woke up every single day by opening up the Word of God and asking Him to speak to you through His Word by the power of the Holy Spirit?

What if, instead of reaching for your phone first thing in the morning, you reached for your Bible? What if, you set your alarm just a few minutes earlier, so you could get into the presence of God and hear from Him?

I guarantee, you would build a habit of craving Him each and every day.

Would you be willing to spend 10-15 minutes each day over the next week to be in the Word of God?

Yes! I, _____, will
give 10 minutes every day for the next week to spend
time in the Word of God.

Signature:

_____

Date: _____

I've found that having a plan in place leads to a more
reliable and consistent "Time Alone with God." So,
let's make a quiet time plan for the next week:

Time: *(7am)*	
Place: *(living room)*	
Tools: *(Bible, journal, devotional)*	
Reading plan: *(The Unwasted Life Daily Reading Plan)*	

The Word of God adds depth to your walk with Christ that you absolutely cannot conjure up on your own or in any other way.

Remember: In order to live a fruitful life, you must connect to the vine daily. Being in the Word of God every single day is one of the surefire ways to remain connected to the vine.

ELIMATING LIFE-WASTERS: WEEK 5: PHYSICAL-WASTERS

This week's fast will be focused on the physical-wasters in our lives. How about we replace our hunger for food with an insatiable hunger for God?

Choose 1 <u>physical-waster</u> to fast for the next 3 days.

Examples: Extra-food, extra-treats, Starbucks, candy, etc.

For the next 3 days, I will fast…

_____

PRAY

Lord, I want to yearn for you. I want to burn with passion over you, and only you. Hungry, I run to you, for I know you satisfy.

God, I crave you more than any other thing.

You are everything to me. Jesus, I need you more. You're all I want. You're all I need.

WEEK 6

THE UNWASTED LIFE

DOES NOT DWELL ON THE PAST

STUDY : : HEAD

But one thing I do: Forgetting what is behind and straining toward what is ahead, I press on toward the goal to receive the prize for which God has called me heavenward in Christ Jesus.

Philippians 3:14

When I was in high school, I ran track. Now let me preface this by confessing, I am *not* a runner! I love sports, but track was my least favorite. My softball and basketball coaches would lovingly yell, "Unhitch the wagon, Lovvorn!" as I ran the bases or ran the court. I was just not blessed with speed, but I went to a small private school where we could play every sport, so I did!

Every year, when track season rolled around, I honestly kind of dreaded it. They put me in the 800 meter race every single year. I guess they knew I most definitely wasn't a sprinter, but I didn't have the kind of endurance to run the really long races, so the 800 meter was the middle ground and most realistic for me.

Although, I am not a talented runner, I *am* extremely competitive. I want to win at whatever I'm competing in, so I ran to win in every single race.

In all honesty, I think we *all* knew that I was never going to win, but I still ran my hardest because I wasn't about to slack off.

And, here's the thing, even though I wasn't ever the fastest or one with the greatest endurance, I still trained, practiced, and ran with all I had. I put everything into every race. And, you know what? My coach knew that I put my all into every practice and every race, and she was proud.

In fact, even though I was never the fastest or most talented on any of my teams, my coaches often named me as the greatest leader. They made me captain. They gave me the "fighting heart" award. Why? Because I gave it my all. I pressed on. I focused all my energies on one thing. I ran to win. And, they noticed that kind of effort. They honored that kind of effort. And, they knew that my effort inspired, encouraged, empowered, and led others to compete with the same effort.

I believe that's what Paul is encouraging us to do here in Philippians 3. He's telling us to pursue, press on, and reach forward with everything in us to lay hold of the prize.

In 1 Corinthians 9:24, Paul urges us to *"run in such a way that you will win."*

As I thought about this phrasing, I was struck by his command to "run *in such a way."* His focus isn't necessarily on the outcome of the race, but His emphasis is placed on the *way in which we run.*

In our pursuit of Christ, we've got to stop looking to the right and left, focused on the talents of others.

When I ran track, if I had gotten so caught up on everyone else's abilities, then I probably wouldn't have run at all. I would have looked at the girls in the lanes next to me and thought, *I don't have a chance.* Instead, I kept my eyes on the finish line, and I ran as if I could win. I gave it my all.

That's all that Christ is calling us to do. Keep your eyes on the prize. Keep your eyes on Jesus, and run to Him with everything in you.

Don't look to the right or left to see how others are running. Don't become discouraged when it looks like someone else is "more capable." All that will do is put you on the sidelines.

Focus on the way you're running. Are you pressing on with everything in you? Are you giving it your all? Are you keeping your eyes on the prize? If so, just like my coach, God will look on you with pride, delighted in the way you have given your all in the pursuit.

READ PHILIPPIANS 3:12-14

Not that I have already obtained all this, or have already arrived at my goal, but I press on to take hold of that for which Christ Jesus took hold of me. Brothers and sisters, I do not consider myself yet to have taken hold of it. But one thing I do: Forgetting what is behind and straining toward what is ahead, I press on toward the goal to receive the prize for which God has called me heavenward in Christ Jesus.

Philippians 3:12-14

What is Paul trying to "take hold of"?

(What is Paul's goal in life?)

_____

_____

_____

_____

> What is the "prize" that Paul is referring to in this passage?

_____

_____

_____

_____

> What did Paul need to forget from the past?
>
> (See Philippians 3:4-6, Acts 7:54-8:1)

_____

_____

_____

_____

THE PAST

"Believers cannot live on past victories, nor should they be debilitated by the guilt of past sins."

– John MacArthur

"Forgetting the past…"

Forgetting the past entails the good and the bad of the past. In Paul's case, he had to lay aside all of his religious accolades and accomplishments, as well as the pain of his sins.

As we discuss "forgetting the past," first, let's examine the negatives of our pasts.

In order to move forward, it is imperative that you lay aside and leave behind the regret, guilt, and shame that slows you down.

READ HEBREWS 12:1-2

Therefore, since we are surrounded by such a great cloud of witnesses, let us throw off everything that hinders and the sin that so easily entangles. And let us run with perseverance the race marked out for us, fixing our eyes on Jesus, the pioneer and perfecter of faith. For the joy set before him he endured the cross, scorning its shame, and sat down at the right hand of the throne of God.

Hebrews 12:1-2

What's the difference between "everything that hinders" and "the sin that so easily entangles"?

_____

_____

_____

_____

Give examples of what may fit in those two categories from your own life.

"Everything that hinders"	"The sin that so easily entangles"

What does it look like to "throw off" these things?

_____

_____

_____

_____

If you're sitting there, thinking, "Trish, you just don't understand *my* past. There's no way my past can be forgotten. I can't move forward from what I've done, who I've been, or what's been done to me."

Before you think that, I just want you to remember Paul's past...

Paul was the man overseeing the murder of Stephen (the first Christian martyr). Paul was the one holding the coats as he watched in approval over this stoning.

Paul tore through the early Christian church like a madman, hungry for blood. When he first converted to Christianity, believers were terrified of him, and he was treated as an outcast by many because of his murderous reputation. He was viewed as one of the grossest terrors to early Christianity, and yet God called *him*.

This is the man urging you to "forget the past." If anyone has the authority to make that statement, it's Paul.

In 1 Timothy 1:15, Paul says:

> *"Christ Jesus came into the world to save sinners--of whom I am the worst."*

Paul owns the title as "the worst of all sinners." So, if the worst of sinners gives you the liberty to *forget the past,* you must do so.

Paul understood the debilitating effects of carrying sin. He knew the dangers of holding on to guilt and shame. He knew the importance of forgetting what

God deemed already forgotten because of the blood of the Lamb.

Clinging to forgiven sins in shame and guilt, as if they are unforgiven, shrinks the power of the Cross and robs God of the glory He deserves.

As Christ-followers, we are commanded to walk in the freedom and forgiveness of the Cross, because when we walk in this freedom and forgiveness, we highlight the power of God in our lives.

But, when we fester in a state of self-pity and penance, we deny God the opportunity to display the work of restoration, redemption, and recreation in our lives.

You must learn to find forgiveness, freedom, and forgetfulness from the past.

I call this kind of forgetfulness "holy-amnesia." The Lord allows us to move forward with a selective memory. We remember His powerful work of restoration, rescue, and redemption, in order to give Him glory for the transformation He has accomplished in our lives. But, we forget the shame, guilt, and regret that once paralyzed us from moving forward in purposeful freedom.

God is so faithful to give us this kind of "holy-amnesia," but we should never forget His provision and deliverance from the past because that part of our story should be used to display the splendor of our God.

I am so grateful that we serve a God who brings purpose from the pain of our pasts.

I wholeheartedly believe that He never allows an ounce of our pain to be in vain.

I've written a book for teenage and college girls called *The Struggle Is Real* (release date TBD). In this book, I tell the real-life stories of girls who have walked difficult roads, but have experience the goodness of God along the way. I sat down face-to-face with every girl in the book as she shared her past with me. Many tears were shed through the interviews, many prayers were lifted, and many praises were proclaimed. These girls shared some of their deepest pains, but every single one of them shared that they found purpose out of the pain by sharing their stories for the betterment of those who will read.

This is what God wants to do with your story, as well. He wants to bring purpose out of the pain of your past. Maybe God is calling you to share your story, so that someone else might be comforted to know that they are not alone. Maybe He's calling you to share the healing, restoration, and freedom you have found in Christ with others who are currently walking that same road.

I am wholeheartedly believing the promises of God from Isaiah 61 for you.

READ ISAIAH 61:1-3

---

*The Spirit of the Sovereign Lord is on me, because
the Lord has anointed me to proclaim good news to the poor.
He has sent me to bind up the brokenhearted, to proclaim
freedom for the captives and release from darkness for the
prisoners, to proclaim the year of the Lord's favor and the day
of vengeance of our God,
to comfort all who mourn, and provide for those who grieve in
Zion—to bestow on them a crown of beauty instead of ashes,
the oil of joy instead of mourning,
and a garment of praise instead of a spirit of despair.
They will be called oaks of righteousness, a planting of
the Lord for the display of his splendor.*

Isaiah 61:1-3

What did the Lord anoint Isaiah to do?

_____

_____

_____

_____

Friend, your past will not be wasted. We do not serve a wasteful God.

Instead, we serve a God of transformation and recreation. A God who can take what was broken and make it whole. A God who can take what once was dark and bring light. A God who takes what was once hopeless and infuses it with hope. A God who can take what was once seemly useless and dead, and create something purposeful and beautifully alive.

And, we, as His children rise as living testaments of His transforming power.

He has taken us who were once in darkness, and he has brought us into the light, and we are here to stand and say, "Yes, my past is full of brokenness. But, my God has come in and He has redeemed. And I will stand here, planted as an oak of righteousness, proof of what God has done to display His Glory."

Friend, your sufferings are never wasted. Nothing goes wasted in the economy of our God.

For a moment, I'd like to transition from the negatives our of pasts to the positives.

For some of you (lucky ones), "forgetting the past" may not refer to a long list of shame, regret, or difficulty. Maybe the past for you means a list of *accomplishments* that you need to leave behind.

Banking on past accomplishments in your walk with God places your eyes on the wrong goal. Banking on the "spiritual accomplishments" of your past leaves you in a state of self-righteousness and self-satisfaction, rather than pressing you forward to gain *more* of Christ and experience more of His satisfying work in your life.

This kind of mentality leads to a complacency in your walk with Jesus. I have caught myself, stuck in this mindset, at different times in my walk with God, so I intimately understand the dangers of this mentality. Here's my one question for you:

Have you plateaued in your spiritual life, because you're holding on to the list of things you've done in the past, rather than pushing forward and believing for even more in the future?

WEEK 6
DAILY READING &
JOURNALING

Each day, answer the following questions as you
journal about the passage for the day:

1. What does this Scripture have to do with this week's
   lesson?

2. In your own words, what is this Scripture saying?

3. How can this Scripture change the way you think?

4. How can this Scripture change the way you live?

Day 1	Read: Philippians 3:12-14
Day 2	Read: 1 Corinthians 9:24-27
Day 3	Read: Hebrews 12:1-3
Day 4	Read: Isaiah 61:1-3

Day 5	Read: Luke 9:61-62
Day 6	Read: Psalm 103:10-12
Day 7	Read: Isaiah 38:17

REFLECT : : HEART

"Behold, it was for my welfare
that I had great bitterness;
but in love you have delivered my life
from the pit of destruction,
for you have cast all my sins
behind your back."

Isaiah 38:17

Have you seen God use the pain of your past for His glorified purpose?

If so, remember how He brought purpose from the pain.

_____

_____

_____

_____

How have you seen the memory of your past hinder you from running the race God has for you?

_____

_____

_____

_____

What from your past, do you need to lay aside and forget through "holy amnesia"?

_____

_____

_____

_____

APPLY : : HANDS

"You can wreck your life by neglecting the past and you neglect your life by an excessive living in the past...

The past is not for fueling and paralyzing regret and disappointment. The past is not meant for fueling anger and grudges. A lot of people use the past for regret and use the past for disappointment and use the past for grudges and use the past for anger. Those are all misuses of the past. That is not what the past is for. God didn't give us the past to make us regretful and to paralyze us with disappointment or rage or grudge. There are positive uses of the past that he did ordain and let me just mention four: gratitude, repentance, faith, and wisdom."

– John Piper

I believe in symbolic actions of faith and belief. I believe in tangible, visual practices that act as memorable declarations of God's work in our lives.

This next action I am asking you to take, will not only act as a memorable confirmation in your own life of what God has done, but it will also act as a statement to the Enemy that you are leaving the past behind. You are drawing a line in the sand. You are nailing the stake in the ground. You are making a bold proclamation that you are moving forward from this point on.

On a separate sheet of paper, write down the top 5 memories/pains/regrets from the past that are weighing you down and hindering you from moving forward.

Now, take that list. Blot out every memory with a red permanent marker, as a representation of Christ's blood covering and eliminating the record of your past.

Throw that sheet of paper into the garbage, because remember as Paul said in *Philippians 3:8:*

"I have discarded everything else, counting it all as garbage, so that I may have Christ."

ELIMATING

LIFE-WASTERS:

WEEK 6: MENTAL-WASTERS

This week's fast will be focused on the mental-wasters in our lives. We often allow our thoughts to paralyze us. The Enemy is a pro at keeping us on the sidelines with lies he spews.

Choose 1 <u>mental-waster</u> to fast for the next 3 days.

What in your life triggers pain, mistakes, guilt, or pride from the past? Fast that trigger in your life this week.

Examples: Secular music, Instagram, Netflix, etc.

For the next 3 days, I will fast…

_____

PRAY

Lord, show me how you can use the pain and the brokenness of my past for your purpose. Help me believe that you never allow any pain to be in vain. Use the scars of my past to tell a story in the present, as I fix my eyes on the hope of the future.

Have your way in my life. I want to marvel at the beauty only you can create from my ashes.

WEEK 7

THE UNWASTED LIFE

LOOKS FORWARD

WITH

A FOCUS ON THE UPWARD CALL

STUDY :: HEAD

Brothers, I do not consider that I have made it my own. But one thing I do: forgetting what lies behind and straining forward to what lies ahead, I press on toward the goal for the prize of the upward call of God in Christ Jesus.

Philippians 3:13-14

I have purposely bypassed discussing the present for a moment, to jump ahead to the future, because I believe that our perspective and our hope for the future dictate the purpose and intentionality of our present days.

Have you ever endured a circumstance, and in the midst of that present moment, you continued reminding yourself that the difficulty or monotony or tedious nature of the present moment was worth it because of the anticipation of what was ahead of you?

I remember sitting in long, boring classes during college, taking notes in dull lectures, studying tediously into the wee hours of the night, all because of my future hope to graduate with a college degree. Why did I press on in the present? Because of the future goal. The future prize.

I remember enduring the long, nine months of pregnancy with joy and intention. How? Because of *the joy* that was ahead of me. The joy of holding my newborn baby girl. The joy of becoming a mother. My hope and expectation empowered me to continue with purpose amidst the backaches, weight gain, swaying emotions, and morning sickness. Every present moment was worth it, because I had a sure and joyful expectation ahead of me. And, not only did I *endure* the present moment, but I *relished* in the present moment. I found purpose and intention in the growth that was occurring because I knew the prize I was gaining. The process was worth the prize.

If we are able to live life with the same expectation and hope for the future, we can not only endure the difficulties with strength, but we can also view our days as an opportunity to develop and mature towards the grand prize we're heading towards.

> After reading Philippians 3:13-14, how would you describe the "upward call of God in Christ Jesus?"

_____

_____

_____

THE FUTURE

"straining forward to what lies ahead…toward the goal for the prize of the upward call of God in Christ Jesus…"

In the last chapter, we looked at the promise of Isaiah 61 for our past. Now, we will examine Ephesians 3:20-21 as the promise for our future.

READ EPHESIANS 3:20-21

"Now to him who is able to do immeasurably more than all we ask or imagine, according to his power that is at work within us, to him be glory in the church and in Christ Jesus throughout all generations, for ever and ever! Amen."

Ephesians 3:20-21

Look up Ephesians 3:20 in other translations of the Bible.

What other words are used to describe "immeasurably more"?

_____

_____

_____

_____

How does God accomplish the "immeasurably more" in our lives?

_____

_____

Here's the problem with a promise like this, I think many of us disqualify ourselves from the "immeasurably more" category. We leave that category to the ones with a "greater" anointing. We leave this category to the "radical" ones.

I think many of us think, "I'll leave the 'immeasurably more' promise to the Christine Caines, Billy Grahams, Beth Moores, Francis Chans of the world. But me? I don't have the platform. I don't have the gifting. I don't, I don't, I don't."

The exact same Holy Spirit that lives within this "elevated category" of believers that we've created in our minds, lives within each and every believer. Every single one of us has access to this kind of power working in our lives. Ephesians 3:20 tells us that God is able to do "immeasurable more" through "*His power at work within us.*" Listen, God is simply looking for surrendered instruments, empowered by the Spirit, for the Kingdom of God. We'll talk in greater depth about the Spirit's power in our lives in next week's lesson.

Here's the main point: If we're going to believe God's "immeasurably more" promise for our future, *we've got to stop self-disqualifying.* We must start truly believing that He can and will do *immeasurably more* with our surrendered lives. The translation of this "immeasurably more" phrase in the Greek is actually: "beyond, beyond, beyond." God can and will do *beyond, beyond, beyond* what you could possibly ask or imagine. When I hear this, I think, "Then, I want to ask BIG." I want to ask for *more*, so I can watch and see how He exceeds my wildest expectations. Yet, we often ask for *less*, doubting that God can really use people like us.

Who are we to doubt this promise? Do you disqualify yourself? We've got to stop self-disqualifying, and we must start believing that God can and will use our lives in ways we could not possibly imagine.

READ COLOSSIANS 1:12

"giving thanks to the Father, who has <u>qualified</u> us to share in the inheritance of the saints in the kingdom of light."

Colossians 1:12

What does the word "qualified" mean to you?

The Greek word for "qualified" (*hikanoo*) means: *to render fit and to equip one with adequate power to perform duties; to make sufficient.*

This same Greek word is used one other place:

READ 2 CORINTHIANS 3:5-6

"Not that we are <u>sufficient</u> in ourselves to claim anything as coming from us, but our <u>sufficiency</u> is from God, who has made us <u>sufficient</u> to be ministers of the new covenant."

2 Corinthians 3:5-6

Listen, this isn't about *us* being able or sufficient or qualified to do "immeasurably more." This is about *Him*! Our lives are always about pointing to Him and saying, "No, within myself, by my own power, by my own abilities, I am *not* qualified. I am *not* sufficient. But, by His grace and through His power, He has *made* me sufficient and qualified. He has rendered me fit to perform the duties of the Kingdom of God!"

For the glory of God, we must stop self-disqualifying. Part of God receiving the glory that He deserves is our willingness to be used by Him. Then, the same thing that was said of John and Peter will be said of us:

"When they saw the boldness of Peter and John and realized that they were unschooled, ordinary men, they were astonished and they took note that these men had been with Jesus."

Acts 4:13

This is why we must not self-disqualify. We highlight the majesty, power, and glory of God, when we allow Him to use our simple, ordinary lives. When people see the simple, the uneducated, the shy, the incompetent, the un   trained, the whatever, become the empowered, the bold, the confident, the qualified for the Kingdom of God, they take note. They're astonishment leads them to the recognition that we have been with Jesus.

Listen: If God says, "You're qualified!" then you're qualified. It does not matter what anyone else says or thinks. His qualification trumps all other disqualifications.

How do I have such confidence in our qualification? Because this is how he qualified us:

READ COLOSSIANS 1:12-14

"Giving thanks to the Father, who has <u>qualified</u> us to share in the inheritance of the saints in the kingdom of light. For He rescued us from the domain of darkness, and transferred us to the kingdom of His beloved Son. God has purchased our freedom with His blood and has forgiven all our sins."

Colossians 1:12-14

> What did God do to qualify you?

_____

_____

_____

_____

> What does it mean to "share in the inheritance of the saints"?

_____

_____

We were once unqualified, but God qualified us by *transferring us* into a new Kingdom. We who were once unqualified are now qualified as His sons and daughters. When He purchased our freedom and forgave all of our sins, He stamped us with a new name. A new qualification. We have been branded as one of His holy people. Marked as a saint. Adopted as a member of the family. *Qualified.*

When we self-disqualify, we reduce and belittle His work of redemption and His payment of freedom on the Cross.

This inheritance is our future. And, get this? Not only is this inheritance part of our future, but it is part of our present. We live our lives in accordance with our new status as His children.

Look forward to the future inheritance. When you do, I believe you'll begin living like you're part of the family. Living in a way that reflects the status of your position as a son or daughter of the King of Kings. When you live with your eyes forward, focused on the upward call, you will find yourself living an unwasted life.

WEEK 7

DAILY READING &

JOURNALING

Each day, answer the following questions as you
journal about the passage for the day:

1. What does this Scripture have to do with this week's
lesson?

2. In your own words, what is this Scripture saying?

3. How can this Scripture change the way you think?

4. How can this Scripture change the way you live?

Day 1	Read: Ephesians 3:20-21
Day 2	Read: Colossians 1:12-14
Day 3	Read: 2 Corinthians 3:5-6
Day 4	Read: Acts 4:13

Day 5	Read: Philippians 1:6
Day 6	Read: 2 Corinthians 4:16-18
Day 7	Read: 1 Corinthians 2:9

REFLECT : : HEART

My purpose outweighs my pain.

My destiny outweighs my history.

My crown outweighs my cross.

My hope outweighs my hardships.

God's Grace outweighs my shame.

The blessing outweighs the burden.

God's favor outweighs my frustration.

— Steven Furtick

READ PHILIPPIANS 1:6

"For I am confident of this very thing, that He who began a good work in you will perfect it until the day of Christ Jesus."

Philippians 1:6

I believe this "perfecting" mentioned in Philippians 1:6, is part of accomplishing the "immeasurably more" in your life. Start asking yourself: "What do I *really* believe God can do in and through my life?"

Do you have the dreams of God in your heart?

What dream(s) has God planted in your heart for the Kingdom of God?

_____

_____

_____

_____

What "good work" has he initiated in you?

_____

_____

_____

_____

Do you believe that He will bring that "good work" to fruition? Why or why not?

_____

_____

_____

_____

How do you minimize or shrink the power and capability of God's work in your life?

List 5 ways that you self-disqualify:

_____

_____

1. _____

2. _____

3. _____

4. _____

5. _____

Who are we to doubt the dreams of God in our hearts? If He has given you a dream or hope for the future with the goal of bringing glory to His name, who are you to doubt His ability to accomplish that dream?

I'm convinced that the dreams and hopes stirring in my heart for the Kingdom of God are just a tiny snap shot into the massive plan that God has for my life and for His Kingdom purposes, and I believe the same is true for you. All you have to do is keep your heart humbly surrendered, and keep your motives Kingdom-focused and God-centered.

He's got more for you than you could possibly imagine. Are you willing to surrender and be used for His Kingdom purposes on this earth? All He's looking for is a surrendered life. A willing vessel, an illuminator of His light, and a carrier of His Good News.

Remember from Week 3: Our one role is to remain connected to the producer. *We* do not produce the fruit, we connect ourselves to the *Producer!* This same principle applies when desiring to live a life that fulfills the "immeasurably more" promise. Your role is to remain connected to the power source of the Christian life – the Holy Spirit. When connected to the power of the Spirit, with your eyes focused on the upward call for which you have been called, you will absolutely experience a life beyond, beyond, beyond what you could ever imagine.

APPLY : : HANDS

"Will you stop focusing on what is wrong with you, and start focusing on what is right with Jesus?"

— Christine Caine

The longer I live, the more I am convinced that our perspective dictates the way we live our current days. If we can change our focus from looking at the past, and shift our focus to Jesus and the call He has on our lives, we absolutely will live eternally significant lives.

If you can take the magnifying glass off of your imperfections, your inadequacies, and yourself, and instead, zoom in with a laser focus on Christ Jesus your Lord, your days on this earth with be unbelievably well spent, extraordinarily Kingdom focused, and astonishingly impactful on eternity. You will look back at the end of your life, and you will be overwhelmed by the way God *really did* keep His promise to accomplish immeasurably more. How? Because you kept your eyes on the prize. You kept your eyes on Jesus.

Dream this week.

Ask God to reveal the unique call He has placed on your life.

"He is able to accomplish immeasurably more than we would ever dare to ask or hope."

List 4 things you're daring to dream, imagine, ask, or hope:

1. _____

_____

2. _____

_____

3. _____

_____

4. _____

_____

As you write out those dreams, do you find yourself doubting?

For each dream, share the doubts and self-qualifications that run through your mind:

1. _____

_____

2. _____

_____

3. _____

_____

4. _____

_____

ELIMATING
LIFE-WASTERS:
WEEK 7: FOCUS-WASTERS

This week's fast will concentrate on the focus-wasters in our lives. Think of the top distractions in your life. What are the main distractions that sway your focus from Jesus Christ?

Choose 1 <u>focus-waster</u> to fast for the next 3 days.

Examples: Social Media, TV, Shopping, Texting, Parties, etc.

For the next 3 days, I will fast…

_____

PRAY

Lord God, help me believe that you can and will do immeasurable more than I could ever ask and imagine.

Give me Christlike confidence, so that I might fight the self-disqualifying tendencies in my heart.

Help me focus my eyes on you, Jesus. Rid my heart and mind of distractions, so that I may keep my eyes on the upward call you have for me.

WEEK 8

THE UNWASTED LIFE

PRESSES ON IN THE PRESENT

STUDY : : HEAD

But one thing I do: Forgetting what is behind and straining toward what is ahead, I press on toward the goal to receive the prize for which God has called me heavenward in Christ Jesus.

Philippians 3:14

THE PRESENT

"I press on..."

"I press on" denotes a prolonged and continual present action. Last week, we discussed our focus and our finish line. This week, we're discussing the way in which we take steps to get there. To "press on" means "to run, to pursue, to seek after earnestly, and to suffer." In our current state, we strain and we press, because we know that persevering in the present is worth the effort to reach the prize.

It's in the "pressing on" that we reach the "immeasurably more" promise of Ephesians 3:20. How do we get to the point where we see Ephesians 3:20 come to fruition? What does "pressing on" look like in the Christian life? Let's look at the verses preceding the Ephesians 3:20 promise:

READ EPHESIANS 3:14-19

When I think of the wisdom and scope of God's plan, I fall to my knees and pray to the Father, the Creator of everything in heaven and on earth. I pray that from his glorious, unlimited resources he will empower you with inner strength through his Spirit.

Then Christ will make his home in your hearts as you trust in him. Your roots will grow down into God's love and keep you strong. And may you have the power to understand, as all God's people should, how wide, how long, how high, and how deep his love is. May you experience the love of Christ, though it is too great to understand fully. Then you will be made complete with all the fullness of life and power that comes from God.

Ephesians 3:14-19

I'm reminded of Philippians 1:6, as I read that last verse that says, "*then you will be made complete...*" Remember what Philippians 1:6 said: *"He who began a good work in you will bring it to completion."* These verses in Ephesians 3 explain how God brings the "good work" to completion. These verses lay out our daily pursuit during our present days.

What four things does Paul pray will happen in the lives of the Ephesian believers?

1. _____

_____

2. _____

_____

3. _____

_____

4. _____

_____

Let's talk in a little more depth about how we might press on to experience the fullness of life and power that come from God:

1. <u>Live empowered by the Holy Spirit.</u> (Ephesians 3:16)

   The Spirit's power at work within us is the means by which we experience the "immeasurably more" in our lives. Here's the thing, we are *all* indwelt by the Holy Spirit, but we are not all *fully surrendered* to the Holy Spirit.

   I know this because throughout Scripture, we are urged to live according to the Spirit, rather than our flesh. We have a choice. We can either allow the Spirit of God's power to work in our lives, or we can live according to our old desires.

READ GALATIANS 5:16-25

Key verses:

So I say, let the Holy Spirit guide your lives. Then you won't be doing what your sinful nature craves. The sinful nature wants to do evil, which is just the opposite of what the Spirit wants. And the Spirit gives us desires that are the opposite of what the sinful nature desires. These two forces are constantly fighting each other, so you are not free to carry out your good intentions. But when you are directed by the Spirit, you are not under obligation to the law of Moses.

Galatians 5:16-18

"But when the Holy Spirit controls our lives…"

Galatians 5:22a

"If we are living now by the Holy Spirit, let us follow the Holy Spirit's leading in every part of our lives."

Galatians 5:25

Have you ever experienced the internal battle of these two forces fighting against each other?

Describe the experience.

_____

_____

_____

_____

Pray, daily, that you would never quench the Spirit, but always be filled with the power of the Spirit. Submit to the control of the Spirit each day.

2. <u>Dwell with Christ by trusting in Him</u>. (Ephesians 3:17)

We don't usually let anyone "make their home" with us, unless we fully trust them. By trusting Christ with our lives, we connect our hearts to His and dwell in His presence daily. Daily fellowship and union with God is the only way to experience the immeasurably more, unwasted life.

> In what area of your life do you need to trust God more?

_____

_____

_____

_____

3. <u>Root yourself in the soil of God's love</u>. (Ephesians 3:17)

Constant reflection on God's great love for us accomplishes this kind of "rooting." When you are rooted in God's love, the circumstances of life have no ability or power to uproot your faith.

Root yourself in the soil of His love by meditating on His demonstration of love you see throughout Scripture.

> How has God demonstrated His love?
>
> (Use Scripture references to point to these actions of love.)

_____

_____

_____

_____

4. Experience His love. (Ephesians 3:19)

    I know this seems similar to the last point, but I believe being "rooted" in His love and "experiencing" His love are actually two different things. The "rooting" occurs when we believe and stand on the promises of God's love. The "experiencing" occurs when our lives display the reality of the promises of His love.

How have you, personally, experienced God's love?

_____

_____

_____

_____

Are you willing to live your days seeking these four pursuits? These four pursuits mark the lives of Kingdom-focused believers. If you will surrender your life to these four pursuits, you will gain an eternally significant life. Remember, as I said last week, "God is simply looking for surrendered instruments."

He's looking for hearts willing to say:

"Here you go, God. My life is Yours."

READ 2 CHRONICLES 16:9

"For the eyes of the LORD range (move to and fro) throughout the earth to strengthen those whose hearts are fully committed to him."

2 Chronicles 16:9

To what is your heart fully committed to, other than God?

_____

_____

_____

_____

READ ISAIAH 6:8

"Then I heard the voice of the Lord, saying, "Whom shall I send, and who will go for Us?" Then I said, "Here am I. Send me!"

Isaiah 6:8

When we think of "being sent" by God, we often think of something grandiose, but God may simply be sending you into your current circumstances and your current surroundings.

As saints, we are "sent" *wherever* we are. We are on mission wherever He has placed us. *We are the sent.*

175

The question is, "Will you live your daily life like one sent out by God?"

_____

Let's talk a moment about the "mundane things of life."

Living in the "mundane" for Jesus, with eternal purpose can be just as powerful, if not more powerful, than living in the "grandiose."

This is where we see a true heart of *faithfulness*. Living a life that will affect future lives and generations for the Kingdom of God starts in the simple, day to day.

Closeness with Jesus in the monotonous tasks of daily life, shows depth in your relationship with Him more than anything else.

My marriage to Sam is not built on the grandiose moments, rather it is built on and proven in the daily commitment and demonstrations of unconditional love.

Yes, our wedding day was magnificent. Our honeymoon was memorable, but without the daily commitment and sacrifice, those grandiose moments would be void of substance. They would only be empty, meaningless spectacles. It's in the faithful moments when my husband does the dishes because I'm overwhelmed that I see the truest of loves. It's in the late nights of changing dirty diapers, it's in the long conversations, it's in the comforting hugs, it's in the drying of my tears…It's in the small, sacrificial moments, that our love is proven faithful and strong.

The same is true of our relationship with God. Our faithfulness is not proven in the grand moments when speaking on a stage. Our faithfulness is not proven through an Instagram picture portraying a Bible and a Starbucks drink. Our faithfulness is proven in the late nights of prayer on our knees. Our faithfulness is proven in the simple acts of kindness that no one sees. Our faithfulness is proven by the tear-stained pages of our Bibles. The faithfulness is proven in the small, unseen moments.

It's in the moments that feel painfully small, that we are refined. These are the moments we gain reliance and dependence on the Holy Spirit's work in our lives. These are the moments we gain substance. These are the moments we gain grit. These current moments build beautiful, messy pictures of real, solid, substantial faith.

I have found, that I can have more Spirit-directed encounters at the grocery store, than on a stage.

I have the opportunity to minister to a worn-out, lonely fellow mom in the halls of our Mother's Day Out, than anywhere else.

This daily abiding and loving Jesus in the "small things" prepares me for and brings substance to any "grandiose moments" He may have for me in the future.

It's the moments that make our days, the days that make our years, and the years that make our lives. Are you missing the moments?

Don't miss *your* specific calling and impact by longing for *someone else's* divinely appointed calling.

The Unwasted Life does not dwell on the past, but presses on in the present to become all that Christ has for us in the future.

Here's one other thing: we need to redefine our misconstrued, worldly definition of "immeasurably more." God's calculation of "immeasurably more" is likely very different than the world's measure of "immeasurably more."

He's operating in the Kingdom system. His method of accounting differs from the world's methods of accounting.

As you clean up after your family, discipline and redirect your children, and nurture their hearts in the name of Jesus, God is applauding you.

As you lead a small group of friends behind closed doors, into the presence of God in your tiny, one-room apartment, the Lord is extremely pleased.

As you make conversation with a random stranger who seems broken, lonely, and lost in your local coffee shop, your Father smiles with delight.

These hidden, unseen acts of empowered living might just be the "immeasurably more" that God has planned for your life.

You might never dream that He would use your life for the Kingdom of God in these seemingly small ways, but you cannot begin to comprehend the ripple effect that occurs in the Kingdom of God.

Your family tree in the Kingdom of Heaven might end up being much larger than you could ever imagine because of one faithful act of obedience empowered by the Holy Spirit.

WEEK 8
DAILY READING &
JOURNALING

Each day, answer the following questions as you journal about the passage for the day:

1. What does this Scripture have to do with this week's lesson?

2. In your own words, what is this Scripture saying?

3. How can this Scripture change the way you think?

4. How can this Scripture change the way you live?

Day 1	Read: Ephesians 3:14-19
Day 2	Read: Galatians 5:16-25
Day 3	Read: 2 Chronicles 16:9
Day 4	Read: Isaiah 6:8

Day 5	Read: Romans 8:35-39
Day 6	Read: Isaiah 43:18-19
Day 7	Read: 2 Corinthians 12:9

REFLECT : : HEART

"The past is not relevant; what matters is making the maximum effort in the present so as to sustain momentum in the future."

– John MacArthur

Do you have a heart fully committed and longing to be sent?

If so, where may God be sending you?

_____

_____

_____

How can you live as someone "sent" in your current circumstances?

_____

_____

What feels small in your life that God might want to use purposefully?

_____

_____

_____

Which one of the four pursuits we discussed, do you need to pursue more fully?

Circle one.

1. Live empowered by the Holy Spirit.

2. Dwell with Christ by trusting in Him.

3. Root yourself in the soil of God's love.

4. Experience His love.

APPLY : : HANDS

"Yesterday is history, tomorrow is a mystery, today is a gift of God, which is why we call it the present."

— *Bil Keane*

In the left column, list the present tasks of your daily life that feel small and unimportant.

In the right column, list ways God can bring purpose to that seemingly small task.

Daily Tasks	Plan for Purpose

Daily Tasks	Plan for Purpose

ELIMATING LIFE-WASTERS: WEEK 8: AGENDA-WASTERS

This week's fast will be focused on agenda-wasters in our lives. I don't know about you, but I often get so distracted and side-tracked by my *own agenda,* that I rarely submit to *God's agenda* for me.

Choose 1 item from your to-do list to fast this week. Clearly, you should not fast imperative responsibilities you must fulfill, but we all have unnecessary items on our to-do lists. Are you willing to submit your list to God, and allow Him to rewrite your agenda this week?

For some of you, this might be a self-care item on your to-do list: a massage, a workout, a manicure, etc. For others of you (likely my perfectionist or OCD friends), this might mean letting go of a task and trusting that the whole world will not fall apart. (i.e. give up doing the laundry one day, and give that time to the Lord…don't freak out. The laundry will be there tomorrow.)

For the next 3 days, I will fast…

_____

PRAY

Lord God, I know that my present moments create my days, the days, create my years, and the years create my life. May my moments point to you, Jesus.

Teach me to be faithful in the smallest, most mundane moments. Build substance and character in the midst of my perseverance, so I might become mature and complete through you alone.

WEEK 9

THE UNWASTED LIFE
IS MARKED BY EVANGELISM,
STIRRED BY A HEART FOR THE LOST

For many walk, of whom I often told you, and now tell you even weeping, that they are enemies of the cross of Christ, whose end is destruction, whose god is their appetite, and whose glory is in their shame, who set their minds on earthly things.

Philippians 3:18-19

Have you ever had the privilege of leading someone to Christ? I can honestly say that there is absolutely nothing in all the world that brings me greater joy than leading someone to Jesus. I can think back on the many conversations that I've had with individuals that have led to their salvation, and every single opportunity I have to lead someone from death to life, from darkness into the light, from hopelessness to hopefulness brings me the most exhilarating, life-

189

giving, purpose-fulfilling encounter I could ever experience.

One story in particular stands out to me. I sat down with a girl on a bench at Mt. Lebanon Encampment in Texas. She was considered an outcast. Odd. Different. An outsider. Those are my favorite kinds of people. I love the outcast. I love the underdog. I love that person, because I know God deeply loves them, and desires for them to know that they are seen and valued.

As I sat down with this girl, I could see the pain in her eyes. Her face was downcast. Her heart was heavy. We began the conversation, with her face glued to the ground. Her voice low and melancholy. We sat on that bench for nearly three hours. We talked round and round about every doubt she had about God and every pain she had experienced.

She shared that no one had ever cared enough to take the time to sit and talk through her questions and doubts. You see, this girl is extremely intelligent. She is remarkably deep. Her Christian parents had been scared by her questions about the faith. They had been stumped by her doubts. They had chastised her for not simply accepting what she had been taught. But, I was willing to listen. I was willing to dig into the hard questions. I was willing to explain that our

God is big enough to handle our questions and our doubts.

At some point in the conversation, the lightbulb switched from off to on. Her heart came alive. Her doubts, spurred by intellect, were replaced with thrilling questions that lit a fire in her soul to know more of God.

By simply taking the time to prove to her that she is seen. She is loved. She is valuable. She is worth the time of wrestling with difficult questions. She was worth it because Jesus Christ proved she was worth it by enduring every ounce of pain on the Cross.

When that clicked for her, everything changed. Her countenance was lifted. A visible darkness from her eyes changed to a gleaming light. Her voice changed from melancholy to delighted and overjoyed.

She and I were overcome with emotion as she prayed to receive Jesus as her Lord and Savior.

I have never been a part of a more tangible transformation than I was that night.

Do you have a willing heart to see the outcast and take the time to speak truth and love into her life?

The Unwasted Life is constantly stirred by a heart for the lost. Not only are our hearts stirred, but we are then *compelled* to share the Good News, because we recognize that we might be the only chance they ever get.

READ PHILIPPIANS 3:18-19

For many walk, of whom I often told you, and now tell you even weeping, that they are enemies of the cross of Christ, whose end is destruction, whose god is their appetite, and whose glory is in their shame, who set their minds on earthly things.

Philippians 3:18-19

Why does Paul weep?

What is the fate for those who are "enemies of the cross of Christ"?

_____

_____

_____

_____

READ ROMANS 5:10

For if while we were enemies we were reconciled to God by the death of his Son, much more, now that we are reconciled, shall we be saved by his life.

Romans 5:10

Have you ever recognized that you, too, were once an enemy of the cross of Christ?

_____

_____

_____

_____

Something shifts in our hearts, when we recognize that *we too* were once enemies of God. We have no right, whatsoever, to look down on unbelievers in contempt. Why? Because we were once in their shoes. We too, were headed down a road straight toward destruction. But God. Two of the most powerful words in Scripture. But God stepped in and poured His grace out on us. Undeserving us. There was absolutely nothing we did to deserve this grace, and yet He offered this free gift of salvation to us – His enemies.

Romans 5:8 tells us that while we were still dead in our sins, Christ died for us. That's how much God loves us! May we never boast in ourselves or find pride in our salvation. There is nothing in us that deserves this kind of free grace.

This outpouring of unmerited grace should compel us to share this grace with everyone we encounter. May we never show contempt for the lost, but always show compassion for the lost. May we be like Paul, who wept bitterly for those who did not know Christ. He understood the reality of their fate. He understood the magnitude of the underserved gift of life God had given to him, and he was obligated to share that gift to anyone who would listen.

My prayer for you is the same prayer for myself: Lord, don't let us waste our lives by missing the opportunity to share the Good News of Christ to those around us.

READ ACTS 20:24

"But my life is worth nothing to me unless I use it for finishing the work assigned me by the Lord Jesus--the work of telling others the Good News about the wonderful grace of God."

Acts 20:24

How did Paul use his life to make it worth something?

_____

_____

_____

_____

READ ROMANS 1:14-17

I am obligated both to Greeks and non-Greeks, both to the wise and the foolish. That is why I am so eager to preach the gospel also to you who are in Rome. I am not ashamed of the gospel, because it is the power of God for salvation to everyone who believes, first to the Jew, then to the Greek. For the gospel reveals the righteousness of God that comes by faith from start to finish, just as it is written: "The righteous will live by faith."

Romans 1:14-17

What is Paul obligated to do?

_____

_____

_____

_____

What is the Gospel?

(as described in Romans 1:16-17)

_____

_____

_____

_____

You, too, are under the exact same obligation as Paul. *The Life Application Commentary* explains it this way:

What was Paul's obligation? After his experience with Christ on the road to Damascus (Acts 9), his whole life was consumed with spreading the Good News of salvation. His obligation was to people of the entire world…We also are obligated to Christ because He took the punishment we deserve for our sins. Although we cannot repay Christ for all He has done, we can demonstrate our gratitude by showing His love to others.

WEEK 9
DAILY READING &
JOURNALING

Each day, answer the following questions as you journal about the passage for the day:

1. What does this Scripture have to do with this week's lesson?

2. In your own words, what is this Scripture saying?

3. How can this Scripture change the way you think?

4. How can this Scripture change the way you live?

Day 1	Read: Philippians 3:8-9
Day 2	Read: Romans 5:6-11
Day 3	Read: Acts 20:24
Day 4	Read: Romans 1:14-17

Day 5	Read: Ephesians 5:15-16
Day 6	Read: Isaiah 12:4
Day 7	Read: Revelation 12:11

REFLECT : : HEART

"God is in the business of strategically positioning us in the right place at the right time, but it's up to us to see and seize those opportunities that are all around us all the time."

— *Mark Batterson*

Our lives are about sharing Christ with a desperate world. This is the primary work that God has assigned to us.

When was the last time you shared the Gospel with someone?

Explain the emotions you felt when you shared the Good News.

What keeps you from sharing the Gospel?

Circle all that apply:

Fear

Don't feel qualified

Lack of training/don't
know what to say

Complacency

Not a strong
Christian/feel like a
hypocrite

Lack of passion or
compassion

Spiritual Laziness

Embarrassed

Afraid I'll lose friends
or relationships

Worried about being
tolerant or politically
correct

When you think of the real fate of unbelievers – a fate
of destruction, separation from God, eternal hell – do
the above excuses matter enough to keep you from
sharing the Good News? Why or why not?

_____

_____

What motivates you to get past these excuses and
instead share the Good News of Jesus Christ?

_____

_____

_____

_____

God plans divine assignments for us each and every
day. Our job is to recognize the opportunities and
make the most of them.

READ EPHESIANS 5:15-16

*"So be careful how you live, not as fools but as those who are
wise. Make the most of every opportunity for doing good in these
evil days."*

Ephesians 5:15-16

How likely are you to make the most of an opportunity that God places in front of you to share the Gospel?

1. Very unlikely

2. Unlikely

3. Possibly

4. Likely

5. Very likely

1	2	3	4	5

APPLY : : HANDS

"God is setting up divine appointments all the time. Only God can make the appointment, but only you can keep the appointment. It's your job to recognize and respond to the God-ordained opportunities that come your way."

— *Mark Batterson*

One of the greatest ways to share the Gospel is by sharing our personal stories of how God has changed our lives.

READ ISAIAH 12:4

In that wonderful day you will sing:
"Thank the Lord! Praise his name!
Tell the nations what he has done.
Let them know how mighty he is!"

Isaiah 12:4

It's difficult for people to combat your own personal story, so being able to articulate what God has done in your life is extremely important.

READ REVELATION 12:11

"And they have defeated him by the blood of the Lamb and by their testimony. And they did not love their lives so much that they were afraid to die."

Revelation 12:11

The word of your testimony holds power to defeat the tactics of the Enemy. The word of your testimony, proclaiming the work of the Lamb, sends the Enemy fleeing.

Take some time to write out your testimony of all God has done in your life.

_____

_____

_____

_____

_____

_____

_____

_____

_____

_____

_____

_____

_____

_____

_____

At some point over the next week, share your
testimony with someone around you.

I, _____, commit
to sharing my testimony with someone this week,
because I recognize that nothing else matters in life
besides sharing the Good News of Christ to a lost
world.

Signature:

_____

Date: _____

ELIMATING
LIFE-WASTERS:
WEEK 9: TIME-WASTERS

This week's fast will be focused on the time-wasters in our lives. If we are called to make the most of every opportunity, then we must rid ourselves of the time-wasters in our lives.

Choose 1 time-waster to fast for the next 3 days.

What in your life keeps you from noticing the opportunities God might be placing in front of you?

Examples: Phone use, TV use, overworking, etc.

For the next 3 days, I will fast...

_____

PRAY

Lord, give me your eyes to see the ordained opportunities you have for me to build the Kingdom of God.

Break my heart for what breaks yours.

Give me a deep, unquenchable love for those who are lost, so I will share the Good News without hesitation.

WEEK 10

THE UNWASTED LIFE
IS FIXATED ON CHRIST'S 2ND
COMING & ETERNITY

STUDY : : HEAD

But we are citizens of heaven, where the Lord Jesus Christ lives.

Philippians 3:20a

When you made Christ your Savior and Lord, your citizenship transferred to an eternal, heavenly citizenship.

Ephesians 2 tells us that before Christ, each one of us was dead and doomed forever. We were living just like the rest of the world with a passport marked with the citizenship of this lost world. But, when we accepted the free gift of salvation through Jesus Christ, He handed us a new passport with a new citizenship. We became citizens of Heaven, heading towards the Kingdom, just passing through on a mission here on earth.

READ PHILIPPIANS 3:20-21

But we are citizens of heaven, where the Lord Jesus Christ lives. And we are eagerly waiting for Him to return as our Savior. He will take these weak mortal bodies of ours and change them into glorious bodies like His own, using the same mighty power that He will use to conquer everything, everywhere.

Philippians 3:20-21

This isn't our ultimate home. This isn't where we belong. Our citizenship is in Heaven. This passage doesn't say, "We *will be* citizens of heaven." It says, "We *are* citizens of heaven."

How should the truth that you are now a citizen of heaven, change the way you live your life on earth?

_____

_____

> What will Jesus do when He returns?

_____

_____

_____

_____

I can hear God pulling me back to Himself constantly, saying: "Don't get too caught up in this world. This place is not your home. There's so much more for you as a citizen of Heaven. Focus on the eternal things."

READ 1 THESSALONIANS 4:13-18

And now, dear brothers and sisters, we want you to know what will happen to the believers who have died so you will not grieve like people who have no hope. For since we believe that Jesus died and was raised to life again, we also believe that when Jesus returns, God will bring back with him the believers who have died. We tell you this directly from the Lord: We who are still living when the Lord returns will not meet him ahead of those who have died. For the Lord himself will come down from heaven with a commanding shout, with the voice of the archangel, and with the trumpet call of God. First, the believers who have died will rise from their graves. Then, together with them, we who are still alive and remain on the earth will be caught up in the clouds to meet the Lord in the air. Then we will be with the Lord forever. So encourage each other with these words.

1 Thessalonians 4:13-18

What encouragement do you find from this passage?

_____

_____

_____

_____

READ REVELATION 22:12

"Look, I am coming soon, bringing my reward with me to repay all people according to their deeds."

Revelation 22:12

> What does Jesus mean when He says: "I am bringing my reward with me to repay all people according to their deeds"?

_____

_____

_____

_____

Let me clarify something: our deeds do not save us. There is nothing we have done to earn our salvation, and there is nothing we can do to lose our salvation. Our salvation is a gift from God through the shed blood of Jesus Christ. Salvation is by grace, through faith, in Christ alone.

But, as believers, the way we live matters. Our lives are significant, and one day we will be judged for the way we lived.

I always ask myself this: "When my life on earth has passed, and I meet Jesus face to face, will He say, 'well done, good and faithful servant'?" Or, could I miss what this life on earth is really all about: Jesus and building His eternal Kingdom.

READ ROMANS 14:10,12

"Remember, each one of us will stand personally before the judgment seat of God...So then each one of us will give an account of himself to God."

Romans 14:10, 12

READ 2 CORINTHIANS 5:10

"For we must all stand before Christ to be judged. We will each receive whatever we deserve for the good or evil we have done in our bodies."

2 Corinthians 5:10

As Christians, our judgement is not a question of condemned or not condemned. We already know that there is _no_ condemnation for those who are in Christ Jesus (Romans 8:1). Our judgement is to determine our rewards, not our eternal destiny. Our destiny is set in stone.

READ 1 CORINTHIANS 3:11-15

"For no one can lay any foundation other than the one we already have—Jesus Christ.

Anyone who builds on that foundation may use a variety of materials—gold, silver, jewels, wood, hay, or straw. But on the judgment day, fire will reveal what kind of work each builder has done. The fire will show if a person's work has any value. If the work survives, that builder will receive a reward. But if the work is burned up, the builder will suffer great loss. The builder will be saved, but like someone barely escaping through a wall of flames."

1 Corinthians 3:11-15

Our foundation in Christ is set. Nothing can cause that foundation of salvation to waver. Every single believer has the exact same, unwavering foundation. But, not every believer uses the same materials. The question will be: *What did you build atop that foundation?*

What does this passage say the fire will reveal?

_____

_____

_____

_____

Unlike unbelievers, whose judgement determines their eternal destiny, the believer's judgement determines his or her rewards. Our judgement will be like a fire that sweeps over the deeds of our lives. The "wood, hay, or straw" of our lives will burn away. These are the things we do and say of <u>no</u> eternal significance. The deeds described as "gold, silver, and jewels" are the deeds that will last. These are the things of eternal significance, and from these deeds we will receive a reward. This fire that will sweep across our lives is the very gaze of Jesus Christ. Revelation 19:12 describes the eyes of Christ as a blazing fire. As we stand before Jesus, face to face, He will look over our lives, and everything will be laid bare. What in your life will withstand the fiery gaze of Christ?

I don't know about you, but I don't want to be saved as one "barely escaping through a wall of flames." I want to build my life wisely. I want a life that shines brightly. I want a life that withstands the fire. I want a life that displays the glorious splendor of my God. I want a life made of gold, silver, and jewels. Don't you?

How about you start living radically on purpose for the Kingdom of Heaven, so that whenever your time comes and you see Jesus face to face, you will *know* that you lived every day for the ordained purposes He laid out for you?

Then, at the end of your life, you can contently and confidently say, "I know I spent my life with Jesus. I lived out the purposes He had for me. I know I took every chance to live *for* Him because I lived *with* Him."

WEEK 10
DAILY READING &
JOURNALING

Each day, answer the following questions as you journal about the passage for the day:

1. What does this Scripture have to do with this week's lesson?

2. In your own words, what is this Scripture saying?

3. How can this Scripture change the way you think?

4. How can this Scripture change the way you live?

Day 1	Read: Philippians 3:20-21
Day 2	Read: 1 Thess. 4:13-18
Day 3	Read: Revelation 22:12
Day 4	Read: Romans 14:10, 12

Day 5	Read: 2 Corinthians 5:10
Day 6	Read: 1 Corinthians 3:11-15
Day 7	Read: Revelation 21:3-7

REFLECT : : HEART

"Bible teaching about the Second Coming of Christ was thought of as "doomsday" preaching. But not anymore. It is the only ray of hope that shines as an ever brightening beam in a darkening world."

– Billy Graham

Are you ready to give an account to Christ of your life? Why or why not?

_____

_____

_____

_____

_____

_____

_____

Take some time to think about your daily actions.
What do you believe fits in the "wood, hay, and
straw" category (deeds of no eternal significance)?
What do you believe fits in the "gold, silver, and
jewels" category (deeds of complete eternal
significance)?

Wood, Hay, Straw	Gold, Silver, and Jewels

Which column is longer?

_____

_____

If you find that your "wood, hay, straw" column is longer, how can you change that?

_____

_____

APPLY : : HANDS

"The second coming of Christ will be so revolutionary that it will change every aspect of life on this planet. Christ will reign in righteousness. Disease will be arrested. Death will be modified. War will be abolished. Nature will be changed. Man will live as it was originally intended he should live."

– Billy Graham

When foreigners become citizens of the United States of America, they are required to declare this Oath of Allegiance:

"I hereby declare, on oath, that I absolutely and entirely renounce and abjure all allegiance and fidelity to any foreign prince, potentate, state, or sovereignty, of whom or which I have heretofore been a subject or citizen; that I will support and defend the Constitution and laws of the United States of America against all enemies, foreign and domestic; that I will bear true faith and allegiance to the same; that I will bear arms on behalf of the United States when required by the law; that I will perform noncombatant service in the Armed Forces of the United States when required by the law; that I will perform work of national importance under civilian direction when required by the law; and that I take this obligation freely, without any mental reservation or purpose of evasion; so help me God."

I have altered this Oath of Allegiance to create a new

oath for those who have been made citizens of
heaven:

The Oath of Allegiance to the Kingdom of Heaven

"I, _____, hereby
declare, on oath, that I absolutely and entirely
renounce and reject all allegiance and fidelity to the
prince of the world, the desires of the flesh, and the
enemies of the Cross of Christ, of whom or which I
have heretofore been a subject or citizen; that I will
support and defend my Lord and Savior, Jesus Christ
and the Word of my God against all enemies, seen
and unseen; that I will bear true faith and allegiance in
the name of Jesus Christ; that I will bear the Sword of
the Spirit and put on the full armor of God on behalf
of my Savior when compelled; that I will perform
humble service and a willingness to suffer for the
cause of Christ; that I will faithfully follow the good
work that God began in me, because I am confident
that He will bring it to completion; and that I take this
obligation freely, without any reservation or purpose
of evasion; so help me God."

Signature:

_____

Date: _____

> # ELIMATING LIFE-WASTERS: WEEK 10: MATERIAL-WASTERS

This week's fast will focus on the material-wasters in our lives. This week, we have recognized that this world is not our home. Our citizenship is in heaven, and we desire to build a life with the lasting and permanent things of eternity, rather than the fleeting, temporary things of this world.

In light of this week's lesson, choose 1 <u>material-waster</u> to fast for the next 3 days.

Examples: Extra clothes, extra possessions, extra food, etc.

> For the next 3 days, I will fast…
>
> _____

PRAY

In the name of Jesus, give me the power to live a life unwasted.

Give me the power and wisdom to fix my eyes on eternity. Open the scope of my vision to see how short this time on earth is compared to eternity in heaven.

Empower me to live a life that is eternally significant.

Jesus, my life is yours, forever and ever.

Amen.

ABOUT THE AUTHOR

Tricia Patterson is a wife to Sam and a mom to a precious and beautiful daughter named Joy. She is a Bible teacher who is passionate about inspiring a younger generation to know Jesus in a personal way. Raised in a Christian home, Tricia accepted Christ at the age of 7, and she received a clear call into full-time ministry at the age of 14. Since that time, she has been teaching teenagers, groups of girls, and young women about her Savior.

Tricia graduated from Baylor University, Magna Cum Laude, with a Bachelor of Arts in Speech Communication. Later, she earned a Master of Arts degree in Christian Education with a concentration in Family Ministry from Dallas Baptist University.

Tricia's greatest joy in life is seeing others come from death to life, from darkness to light, through the saving work of Jesus Christ. She longs for others to find and experience the true life that only comes through Christ and Christ alone.

Website: www.TriciaPatterson.com
Connect with Tricia on a daily basis:
Blog: www.TriciaPatterson.com/blog
Instagram: @TLPat
Twitter: @TrishLPatterson

Made in the USA
San Bernardino, CA
30 November 2017